LIVING AN ARMED LIFE

LIVING AN ARMED LIFE

A Woman's Guide to Adapting Her Carry to
Her Changing Life

Lynne Finch

SKYHORSE PUBLISHING

Skyhorse Publishing books may be purchased in bulk at special discounts for sales promotion, corporate gifts, fund-raising, or educational purposes. Special editions can also be created to specifications. For details, contact the Special Sales Department, Skyhorse Publishing, 307 West 36th Street, 11th Floor, New York, NY 10018 or info@skyhorsepublishing.com.

Skyhorse® and Skyhorse Publishing® are registered trademarks of Skyhorse Publishing, Inc.®, a Delaware corporation.

Visit our website at www.skyhorsepublishing.com.

10 9 8 7 6 5 4 3 2 1

Library of Congress Cataloging-in-Publication Data is available on file.

Cover design by Tom Lau
Cover photo credit: Lynne Finch

Print ISBN: 978-1-5107-0983-6
Ebook ISBN: 978-1-5107-0984-3

Printed in China

For Jim,
Thank you for your support and encouragement
and for being all that you are.

Table of Contents

Foreword

I first "met" Lynne Finch in the blogging world several years ago. We were both fairly new gun bloggers, and much of our material complemented each other. Comments on each other's blogs flowed back and forth, and a friendship was born.

She references an incident in this book about breaking her foot. What she did not mention was that she attended SHOT Show (Shooting, Hunting, Outdoor Trade Show—a trade-only show for the firearms industry) with said broken foot. I saw her during registration (the boot cast gave her away) and flagged her down for our first in-person meeting after a couple years of electronic communication.

What I have learned about Lynne since that time is that she is passionate about shooting and teaching others to shoot. She is fearless in her pursuits. When Lynne was first contemplating National Take Your Daughter to the Range Day, I was in awe. I mean, who thinks of things like that—*and then is able to pull it off?* Truly, when she sets her mind to something, by God, she's going to achieve it.

Her first three books were well received and chock full of information presented in easily digestible pieces. Whereas many books about self-defense and shooting are nothing more than chest-pounding testosterone fests, Lynne's books take a common-sense approach to self-defense. When reading them, you feel as though you are having a conversation with her.

This fourth book is no different. She presents information that can be applied at any stage of life. I had to figure a lot of this information out for myself when I was a young, gun-carrying mother. There just weren't any resources available twenty-some years ago, and many of the suggestions in this book were ones that I had to figure out by trial-and-error. Oh, how I wish I'd had this resource then.

There are a lot of books on the market geared toward women's self-defense. There are even a few books that address self-defense for people with disabilities (temporary or permanent). But there are fewer books that acknowledge the uncertainty or loss of feeling safe, while giving real-life examples on how to regain that feeling. This book is one of those few.

What strikes me about this book is that Lynne expresses what many of us "gun folk" feel: If you are not absolutely certain you can shoot someone to save yourself or your family, then maybe you should look at alternative ways to keep safe. Instead of just stating that, though, Lynne then goes on to discuss the various options to do so; this is not a "gun solves everything" type of book. I am grateful for that, and I am certain others will be thankful as well.

—C. S. Wilson, "GunDiva"
www.thegundivas.com

Introduction

So many of us go through life ill-prepared for the wolf at the door. This is especially true for women.

Now, before everyone gets offended by that, let's look at a few statistics. According to our own U.S. Department of Justice statistics (2014), in 2013, nearly half of all crime victims were female. The bulk of these victims were between the ages of eighteen and forty-nine. Why is this important to know? Because it gives some perspective. This is the age range when many women are new college students away from home for the first time, out and about with our friends, our families, and relaxing at home. Indeed, this is the age where it's sometimes our first foray truly away from protective parents. Same goes for new young mothers in this age range, who are active and on the move with shopping, day care, school drop-offs, and more.

Often we think the bad things in the world won't happen to us, that someone else will fall victim. Think about all those interviews you see on TV when a tragedy strikes. How often do you hear a local being interviewed who says to the camera, "We never thought it would happen in our town, in our own backyard." Unfortunately, most victims feel the same way, even those in large cities, and especially those who feel they live in "safer" neighborhoods. "This just doesn't happen here," they'll say, crime scene tape flapping around the telephone poles behind them.

Well, "this" does happen. I once had complications after surgery. It was a rare complication, and I asked my doctor what the odds were that this could have happened. He looked at me and said, "For you, it was 100 percent." That got me thinking. What *are* the odds? Well, if nothing happens, zero! If it does, though, that doctor was right, its 100 percent.

When it comes to defending yourself in a world where "this" happens, do you know what to do if the worst happens? Have you made a plan to work with those worst-case scenarios? Do you train for those plans?

I do. I plan, I train, and then I teach and coach about it—and now I'm putting it all into this book.

This book is written with you in mind, whether you're a young woman, a mom or, like me, a woman who's getting older (and a little achy and perhaps a bit slower, too). Much of the advice you'll find in these pages is focused on particular needs based on situations specific to women at different stages of your life. For instance, and generally speaking, you have different needs as a young mother in your mid-twenties than you do as a fifty-something mom whose hips are a bit arthritic and whose kids have flown the coop. But, regardless what stage of life you're in, it's important to remember the title of the book—*Living an Armed Life*, emphasis on the "armed."

I'm assuming the "armed" is the probable reason you picked up this book in the first place. You're not alone, though you are at the head of the class, so to speak. It's a relatively new phenomenon in our culture that women are more often armed now—even newer that, when part of a couple, women are carrying right alongside their partners. Nothing wrong with that. In fact, there are lots of things *right* with that, because aside from all the trite things you'll hear about "women's empowerment," the bottom line is that it's important to be able to defend yourself and your family, with or without backup from your other half.

I hope you never need the information here, and that you are at "zero" when it comes to the chances of bad things happening to you. But, should you find yourself in the middle of becoming the other side of that statistic, I also hope that you have taken heed of the advice here and that it is helpful for you.

—Lynne Finch

Part I
A Mindset for Self-Defense

1. Making the Choice

The decision to live an armed life isn't an easy one, and your views about how, when, and where to be armed may change over time, but one of the most important things to remember about that decision is that it is a *choice*. You *choose* to be armed—or not. When you make that choice to be armed you are accepting that you are carrying a weapon—especially if it's a firearm or knife—that has the potential to cause death or serious injury to another human being.

No, You Can't Just Whip it Out And Expect it to End Well

This choice to live armed is not one to be taken lightly, especially with a firearm, which will be the focus of this book. (A note: Yes, there are many other defensive tools out there, and we'll take a look at them in later chapters, but unless otherwise stated, I'll be talking about firearms for defensive use). I've had students who were cavalier about this choice to carry a firearm. I could tell they were thinking, "I can just show the gun to a bad guy like they do on TV and he will back off." Well, he might. Or he might not. What's the bad guy carrying?

What stake in the game does he have? Is he betting you're too chicken to use your gun or aren't skilled enough to make a shot that turns the tables? You don't know the answers to these things, so there's no way to guarantee how an already bad situation will go if you think merely whipping your gun out of your purse or holster or nightstand or glove compartment will do the trick.

But it goes beyond that. If you are considering carrying a firearm for your own protection, you must, *must* be prepared to use it. You must get your mind wrapped around the thought that you might have to take the life of someone else or, at the very least, seriously injure them—and you have to think you can do that in the defense of your own life or the life of a loved one, have to believe that your life, when it comes right down to it, is more valuable than the thug opposite your muzzle trying to do you or your loved one bodily harm.

Not everyone will do the thinking to get to that important decision. Nor will everyone who takes the time to think through the process decide they can risk taking the life of another, even if it means saving their own. And that's okay! Repeat after me:

If you cannot say to yourself that you are prepared to defend your life by any means necessary, including a firearm, then don't carry one—period.

Thinking Gets You to the Choice

I'm going to emphasize again that this mindset, this decision to understand and commit to the possibility of taking someone else's life, is one you need to make *before* you choose to carry. You need to know what you are prepared to do before you walk out of your home with a firearm, before you stash one in a quick-access safe in your nightstand, before you secure and hide one in your home in the event of a home invasion, before the dozens and dozens of ways you may carry or conceal a firearm in the event bad things happen.

Now, some of you reading this are likely thinking that anything can happen to you when a bad situation starts going down. "Freezing" is probably the thing most people think will happen, that they will be unable to pull the trigger when they need to. That's a legitimate concern—but it's *less* of one if you have thought about the things that can happen to you and what you could do in response.

That's what the police and military do. They train all the time for worst-case scenarios, even though they don't know what they're going to do until they're in the middle of a situation. Where they're ahead is that they've thought about how different situations can go and they've trained to address those situations. That goes a long way towards keeping the odds in their favor. They are, in a word, prepared.

You have to be too. In a moment of panic during an attack, adrenaline pumping and all sorts of physiological phenomena happening—tunnel vision, selective hearing, etc.—your brain cannot process the question of *whether* you will fight or submit, draw and use your gun or not. You must be committed *before* a situation escalates. To do less can be fatal for you, and perhaps innocent bystanders.

I went through that decision-making process, just like most people who carry a firearm as they go about their day or decide to keep one handy at home. My choice was in response to a direct and specific threat. Others make the decision to carry or keep a firearm for self-protection as a caution against a rising lack of regard for life by violent thugs who, with all the information we receive these days at a lightning-fast pace, seem to be just about everywhere—they know the "it" and "that" *can* happen to them, even if it hasn't yet and even if those situations are unlikely. The increased threat of terrorism also plays an increasing part in firearms for self-protection these days, while for others it's just the normal shifts in lifestyles—becoming a spouse or a parent, for instance—that ups the desire to take the best care they can of the ones they love.

Practice—It's Not Just About Paper Targets

Whatever reason it is that has you arriving at the decision to carry a firearm, you have things in common with all the others who have made a similar choice. First, you all have commitment. You have *committed* to using your firearm for defensive purposes only (when not on the practice range). You have *committed* to knowing and understanding the laws in your area and any areas you might travel to regarding where, when, and how you can carry, and you stay on top of these laws to notice when they undergo periodic adjustments so that you can make the appropriate adjustments to your carry. Last but not least, you have *committed* to practice, practice, and more practice.

The emphasis on practice is deliberate. Shooting is a perishable skill, so, in order to maintain proficiency, you need to practice. Doubt me? Take six months off from a sport you participate in and at which you are good. What happens when you go back to that sport? Besides sore muscles, you probably didn't live up to your previous level of performance.

Let's talk a little bit more about practice. Say, for instance, you play tennis. When you practice, you don't hit balls only from the center of the fault line, do you? No, you take them on the run up close to the net, speedballs from the side, and high overhead lobs from mid-court. Effective practice with a firearm should be approached the same way. That means you have to be committed to more than going to the range and shooting twenty-five rounds at a round paper target from the fifteen yard line while standing still and taking your sweet time. *Much* more. You'll need to practice shooting one-handed (including your weak hand, because what do you do if your strong hand is injured?), and shooting from standing, kneeling, and prone positions. You should practice shooting from uncomfortable positions, from behind and around cover, and from all sorts of distances and angles. You should practice drawing from your holster and retrieving your gun from its safe. You'll also need to practice reloading your firearm and clearing a malfunctioning gun.

The good news is that all this practice is a ton of fun! And heck, it doesn't even have to cost you live ammunition all the time. I'm talking about dry-fire practice at home, either with a completely unloaded gun (I'll cover more on this later), or, like me, you can use a "blue gun" (a dummy firearm that's completely inert and has no moving parts) or an SIRT, short for "shot indicating resetting trigger," another kind of dummy training "gun" that emits a laser but uses no live ammunition. These are great tools for safely practicing the art of shooting around barriers or hitting the ground and drawing from your holster, and they're also useful for practicing in your own home, when you can't make it to the range.

Another tool I use to train with is a body opponent bag (BOB). With BOB I practice delivering physical strikes, backing up and drawing my firearm, or falling backward and drawing (either my actual carry gun completely unloaded, a blue gun, or an SIRT gun). Don't forget to simulate firing

SIRT (shot indicating resetting trigger).

Blue gun.

when using any of these tools. Go ahead, say "bang" out loud while you're pulling the trigger on your unloaded gun and the SIRT tool, and also while pulling a non-moving trigger in a blue gun. It makes a difference and better prepares you for your time on the range and live-fire practice.

During any training of this kind, you must remember to keep your finger straight across the trigger guard and not through it and on the trigger until you're actually ready to "fire." Repeatedly training this way not only ensures you're adhering to one of the basic rules of gun safety, such discipline can help prevent an accidental or premature discharge of your firearm when you're in the middle of an emergency situation and the adrenaline's pumping.

You need to practice for the real world. Practice makes habit, so what you practice is what you will most likely do when the need arises. If you are able to take advanced training that includes firing under stressful conditions, such as someone

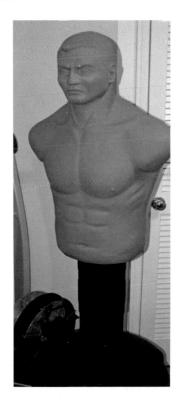

If you are not using a training dummy gun, but instead a real firearm that you intend to carry, it is essential that you ensure that it is unloaded, that no ammo is in the room in which you are practicing (this includes loaded magazines for semi-autos and moon clips or speedloaders for revolvers—all must be removed from your dry-fire area), and that you always aim your practice shots at the safest wall available. Remember, even a gun you've double-checked as being unloaded should always be treated as if it were loaded—always.

screaming at you, someone forcing you to shoot on the move, and even training that includes combat tactics that don't involve a firearm—your hands and feet, pepper spray, knives, etc.—then do it! You can learn a lot from books—many techniques are addressed in my previous book, *Female and Armed*—but nothing takes the place of live training.

I've Made the Choice. Now What?

Choosing to carry a firearm for self-defense involves more than just that initial decision, of course. Indeed, there should be a ripple effect of other decisions that you will need to think through, and some hard truths you'll need to acknowledge, before you make that all-important purchase and start to carry every day.

If you have asked yourself the tough questions—Is my life important to me? Am I willing to defend myself even if it means taking someone else's life?—and answered them in the affirmative, you have to also walk the very fine line of realizing that even if you are prepared to take someone else's life, that will *never* be your goal or intention. "Never shoot to kill, shoot to stop the threat," is a mantra many good shooting instructors use to help make this distinction. This is not Hollywood—there's no line in the script of the "it" that might happen to you, where you will tell the police or the press or your lawyer that you deliberately meant to kill someone. If someone attacking you or a loved one happens to die as a result of your self-defense actions, well, so be it, but that should be a result that's *incidental*, not deliberate.

This is one of the reasons so many instructors start out their self-defense students by having them shoot at the NRA

B-52 target, that life-sized rendition of a human torso and head. Using that target, instructors with new students will have them aim for the center of the torso. Why? Because it's a *big* portion of the target, and one far easier to hit than the head portion. Known as the high center chest, or golden square, the center chest, (roughly clavicle to sternum and outer rib side to side) this is a large target, likely to yield a significant impact to stop the threat. The head is a small space, and depending on distance and caliber, you run the risk of the bony structure of the skull stopping the bullet. The headshot is best saved for when it is essential because something is blocking the torso, such as a hostage. Under stress you are more likely to miss the small shot, but should practice for it. The high center chest is a hit anywhere in the square, and you can shoot faster, delivering more rounds. The head is a smaller target and the most effective aim point is the nose.

Now, all this doesn't mean you go the other direction and intentionally wound someone, either. You will not go all James Bond on someone and shoot the gun or knife or whatever they have out of their hand. You will *always*, if the need arises, take a serious, potentially lethal shot, one you hope will stop the aggressor from coming at you or stop an attack in progress. At the same time, you have to be cognizant of the fact that one shot may not stop someone coming after you. *You have to be prepared to shoot to stop the threat.* You shoot until they stop coming at you.

I'm going to dispel another myth of self-defense. You may have heard an old-timer in a gun store or someone in a bad movie advising someone to "shoot 'em in the leg and they'll be down." Maybe, maybe not. And shooting someone in the leg sure doesn't guarantee they can't still shoot back at you! Such a wounded individual is still potentially very dangerous.

Know that a deliberate wounding puts you at risk for adverse legal action. I'll talk about the aftermath of a shooting near the end of this book—another level of the thinking and preparation process—but you're going to have to answer questions about an intentional "wounding." Did you do it on purpose because you were angry, had a vendetta, or some other reason? In the event of a shooting by you in your own self-defense, you do not want to cast doubt that you were doing anything *but* defending yourself.

Finally, if all that isn't enough to convince you that "shoot 'em in the leg!" is horrible advice, consider that, like the head on that B-52 target, a human leg is a small, narrow target, especially when your adrenaline is pumping, your heart is racing, and your hands are shaking. That makes a successful intentional wounding unlikely.

Center mass is the shot you'll most likely take if the need arises. Still, it's not a guarantee that such a target will present itself or that you'll be able to stop an attack with a shot to the torso. So, let's flip-flop some of this for a minute. What if you take a high center chest shot at an attacker and there's no reaction? It's possible he might be wearing body armor. What if you're being fired upon by an attacker who's behind a barricade, and the only portion of that attacker that's revealed to you is their head? Your options for stopping an attack get narrow in these cases, and fast—and you still have to be committed to stopping the attack if you want to survive.

Gun or No Gun, Have a Plan

I know people who are awesome range shooters, but they do not carry a firearm daily or have one handy at home for self-defense purposes. For many of these recreational shooters, they looked inside themselves and knew they couldn't shoot someone. If that describes you, I encourage you *not* to have a firearm accessible outside use on the range, to lock them away when not in use for sport. By resisting that access, you greatly reduce the risk of having those firearms used against you. How could that happen? Because you decided you could *not* use a firearm to defend yourself and therefore did not *practice* for an event in which you needed to do so, an attacker has an upper hand. You don't know what you're going to do, but he knows what *he's* going to do, and that's get the better of you.

If you have chosen not to keep a gun for self- and home-defense purposes, and even if you have, I do encourage you to take classes in self-defense that don't involve firearms. You should also reinforce your home and learn to use non-lethal defensive tools. Just because you've made the decision not to use a gun for self-defense doesn't mean the bad guy made the same choice. Have a plan.

Whatever your decision, and however long it takes you to make that decision, you must keep in mind that a gun is not a good luck charm. Simply having one will not stop bad things from happening to good people, just as simply showing your gun to a bad guy is no guarantee it'll send him packing. You need to be prepared, and you'll need to think about your gun—how, when, and where you're carrying it, where and how it's stored, and how you'll access it when needed—all the time. But understand that this kind of thinking is a *process*.

A friend who worked retail once told me that, with new gun owners, she explained that keeping a firearm for self-defense and learning to think about it was a lot like learning to drive a car as a teenager. For a while, months usually, but even the first couple years after getting their first license and taking to the road regularly, new drivers will consciously and deliberately go through the step-by-step process of seatbelt on, seat adjusted, mirrors adjusted, radio volume down, check all the mirrors twice, then carefully back out or pull out while looking around all the time. After a while, after those new drivers have some experience behind the wheel and miles on the tires, they're still going through that process, but it's more automatic, and that progresses until they're truly experienced drivers who reflexively, almost unconsciously go through the process they once had to think about in a step-by-step manner. Learning to carry a gun for self-defense or keeping one in the home works the same way.

Shooting is Your Last Resort

Despite my emphasis on shooting skills and the decision-making process, I want to be very clear about one thing: pulling the trigger should be your last resort in a dire situation.

There are many things in a life-or-death situation that will require fast assessments and decisions, but your primary consideration is to determine if you are in danger of bodily harm and, if so, whether pulling the trigger the *best* way to stop that aggression. If you decide yes, then you also have to consider who may be with and/or around you when an attack happens. For instance, most parents don't hesitate when it comes to protecting their children, but what about a random stranger in the street being attacked? What will being a Good Samaritan cost you? You also have to consider innocent bystanders. What do you do if you're being attacked but you don't have a clear shooting path to stopping the attack without wounding or potentially killing someone *not* involved in the attack? Hard question to answer, that one. Even lawyers would struggle with it.

Finally, you have to consider that your primary obligation in any situation might be, maybe even *should* be, to get *away* if possible. Can you retreat and, if so, where do you go and how do you get there? Yes, some states and locales have "stand your ground" laws, which, loosely translated, means that if you're going about your business in a legal manner, you have a right to be wherever you are and defend that position. Other states do not have those laws, thereby more or less *obligating* you to retreat first if possible. But even if you do have a "stand your ground" law to back you up, you still have to ask yourself, what is *your* first obligation? In other words, is it better to retreat and *not* become engaged in a situation that could escalate to the taking of lives, or does your "right" to be where you are supersede a moral obligation to retreat?

For most of us who instruct and work with firearm self-defense on a daily basis, we emphasize that anyone who carries needs to employ every skill, ounce of awareness, and ingenuity to *minimize* the need to draw your gun. A fight avoided is a fight won.

After a Self-Defense Shooting

There is a saying, "When you pull the trigger, two lives are changed forever." If you become involved in a life-or-death confrontation and you are forced to use your firearm in self-defense, it's important to understand that your life will never be the same. You can count on legal and civil repercussions, even if it is eventually proven and acknowledged publicly that you acted in self-defense. There are also the very real repercussions you'll experience as a result of public perception—some will support you, some will chastise you, some may call you a hero, and some may sue you. There's also a strong probability that you will be injured in such a dire attack. But even if you escape without harm to yourself, you will always live with the memory of pulling the trigger, and despite knowing that you were within your rights to do so, you may have significant psychological issues to work through.

Is this worth it when weighed against the risk of death from an attacker? For me, that answer is "yes." Now it's time for you to decide.

2. When to Carry

You might be surprised how often instructors get the question, "When should I carry my gun?" Well, the best answer is whenever you legally can. Why? *Because you never know what will happen.*

I was once asked why I carried my gun to go grocery shopping. The answer was easy. I said, "If I was going someplace where I thought I would *need* a gun, why would I go there? I don't deliberately go to dangerous places hoping I might get attacked and get a chance to shoot someone. That would be foolish—and dangerous. There are no guarantees how something like that would end, and I don't have hundreds of thousands of dollars to spend on a legal defense—that, and I have no *desire* to shoot someone. I'm quite happy with paper and steel targets, thank you."

I've had the "when to carry" question sometimes propositioned as "Why carry at all?" One of the best responses I've ever heard to that question goes something like this:

> Them: So why do you carry?
> Me: Do you keep a fire extinguisher near your kitchen stove?

Them: Sure.

Me: Well, are you expecting a fire?

Them: Well, no, but you know, it's there just in case.

That usually gets them. You can almost see the light bulb come on.

Still, the question is pervasive, and it is one you should ask yourself and think about. Take a look at recent history, for instance. Many places have become gun-free zones. And where do criminals and mentally ill persons with a desire to shoot a lot of people go? You guessed it: gun-free zones. There's no real added consequence for them; they're already willing to break the law, what's one more?

That said, I prefer to go places that allow me to legally carry a concealed firearm (we aren't going into the open-carry debate here). That way I know I have a choice and options.

I recently went to the first weekend showing of a new action movie. I'd never seen an **IMAX** movie and didn't realize how much the bass in the theater would reverberate down to my toes. It reminded me of the feeling of sitting in the stands at stock car race as a kid, where you could feel the vibration from the cars as they whizzed past you. Like many theaters, the one I chose had been declared a gun-free zone, so I wasn't armed. I barely made it through the movie. Between the action on screen, the volume thundering its vibrations through my body, and the memories of theater shootings in the news, it took a lot for me to stay. I think, ultimately, I refused to leave because when terrorists or criminals cause you to change your behavior, they win. In the end, I loved the movie, but was drained by the level of tension sitting there.

All this brings me to another point. With the plethora of gun-free businesses, schools, courthouses, and other premises that abound these days, you must not only be cognizant of those zones, you'll have to think about ways to work around them as you go about your daily life as a woman carrying a firearm. Maybe you pick up your child a block from the school instead of in front, so you're out of the gun-free zone while you carry. Maybe you switch grocery stores or movie theaters, or frequent other businesses that don't specifically prohibit concealed carry. There's not much you can do about entering a courthouse or other government building these days while carrying, but you can make the added effort to, say, safely secure your firearm in your car and park it off government property so that it's available to you the minute you get back in your vehicle. Who knows, that extra five minutes it took you to walk to your destination and back could very well save your life.

3. Integrating Family and Friends into Your Concealed Carry Thinking

When you are outside the home and carrying (let's again assume concealed) it is my opinion that those with you need to know you're carrying so that they can respond appropriately if a confrontation arises. These people could be a spouse, your children, or friends.

Why have this discussion? Primarily because it can be worked out in advance how each in your party can protect the others (especially if more than one of you is carrying). You can also determine who would be the first to respond with a firearm if more than one of you are carrying, and you can also establish how to communicate with each other in a dire situation so that the danger to each of you is minimized. Some trainers are now offering classes for couples that address this last issue.

Communication between a couple or within a small group when a life-or-death situation is occurring must be quick and concise, and each member of your party must be aware of exactly where the others are so that they can be kept out of the line of potential fire from within your party. For family members and friends who routinely travel and gather together and also carry, it is recommended that you practice what to do with some informal drills. Let's look at an example.

Kid-Tested, Mother Approved

Say you're out for a stroll or a bike ride with your kids. What do those children do if you are confronted with someone who demands money from you in an aggressive manner or you're otherwise accosted? Many parents say they will push the kids behind them. Ok, that's fair, most parents would instinctively protect their children in this manner. But what does that do to you, the parent? For one, it splits your focus, making it harder for you to move without the risk of tripping over a frightened child. It also puts the kids in danger simply because they are only behind you, but still in the immediate vicinity of the problem at hand.

In thinking through this situation, it would be better to have a code word, similar to a code word to pick them up from school, that tells the children to scatter in different directions (or simply away, for the single child) and hide (older children could possibly be instructed to get help if possible). That scattering should include instructions for the children to run away at angles from you—not straight away behind you, but to the sides—being mindful of traffic, then seek a good hiding place and stay there until you or law enforcement call for them to come out. This puts them out of harm's way and frees you to focus on dealing with the attacker (who most likely isn't interested in the kids anyway). This kind of tactic also makes it harder for a criminal to use a child—grabbing them, intimidating them, etc.—in an effort to gain your compliance.

Now, you don't want your kids to be terrified every time you take them out for that walk, don't want them to think there's a bad guy hiding around every corner. So make a game of it, much like the school does when teaching about stranger-danger. "Kids, let's pretend . . ." as you're walking, surprising them with the secret word at some point and watching (and helping them) scatter and hide. Think of it as similar to a fire drill. You practice so that, in an emergency, they know exactly what to do without hesitation. Make it a game, and they will remember what to do if they ever need to.

Training Your Adult Friends

Your unarmed adult friends, when you are going about daily life armed, can be educated to react to a threatening situation in a manner very similar to the way you'd teach children. Unless one of them has been educated in self-defense tactics at the Krav Maga level, make sure they understand that they need to be behind you and to the sides—because you can trip over an adult just as easy as you can a child—if you are the one in the group carrying and you are attacked. Also, while they may not run and hide, (depending on the situation), they should understand that they will need to give you a wide berth and always be behind your line of fire in the event things escalate to that level.

Carrying in the Home

Think a home invasion can't happen to you? Listen to the evening news for a week or so and you'll see it happened to someone: someone in the big city, someone in the suburbs, and someone *waaaaay* down that long, desolate dirt road in rural South Dakota. Still not convinced? Google "reported home invasions" then take a few hours to scroll.

It can happen. It does happen. Have a plan, even several plans, for coping with a home invasion. What happens if you're broken into through the front door and you're in the kitchen or den? What if it's the back door and you're upstairs putting the kids to bed? Do you have a safe room with a firearm, a phone, and a good lock on the door? If you have children, do you make their room your safe room and, if so, how do you safely secure a firearm there for emergency use by you or another authorized adult? Do your kids even know what to do if there's a break-in while everyone is home? What if everyone's in different rooms of the house when an invasion happens? What if everyone's in bed? (The trusty baseball bat or golf club under the bed can buy time if used by one while the other goes for the gun.) Do you, should you, and can you evacuate from your home and, if so, have you designated a rendezvous point nearby where you know to gather to do a head count and get the family to safety? Have you discussed how to deal with police entering the house while you're barricaded in a safe room so that you don't injure one of them?

The choice to keep a firearm in your home, whether you use those firearms for sporting purposes, collect them, use them for self-protection, or all of the above, is a serious responsibility. Gun owners must be committed to obtaining the appropriate training and having a clear understanding of safe handling and storage rules if they hope to achieve the intended personal safety benefits. But when it comes to storing them in your home in anticipation of using them there for defense, ask yourself these questions:

- Are my security concerns realistic and consistent with local crime rates?
- Do other adults in my household support maintaining a gun in the house?
- Will other adults with access to the firearm join me in a firearms training and safety program?
- What precautions will I practice to safeguard children?
- Is there any mental illness or drug and alcohol abuse within the members of the household?

Your decision to store a gun in the home for home defense should also take into consideration issues such as the individual temperaments of those in the household, their known or anticipated reactions to emergency situations, and other specific family circumstances that may affect both your

That sudden bump in the night.

Ready to meet an intruder?

decision to have a gun in the house at all, as well as how you'll handle one in a dire situation if you do choose to keep one.

Precautions When Carrying

Carrying a gun is a way of life for a lot of people. After all, you never know when you might need one. But there are things to consider, and be prepared for, when you carry on a regular basis.

Not every business, and especially not most government offices these days, will allow you to carry a firearm into the building. It is your responsibility to know where you can and cannot carry. Generally, most shopping malls have a posting somewhere (even it if is often in very small print) that states that store management prohibits weapons on the premises. Post offices, airports, and government buildings like courthouses almost always prohibit weapons. (You can, of course, transport a firearm on a plane as checked baggage with most airlines, but you cannot carry concealed onto the airport grounds. Always consult with your airline regarding their requirements for flying with firearms.) What's the difference if you violate the law of the land from one side to the other? Carrying in the shopping mall, in most cases, might get you a trespass charge. Carrying in a federal building can be a much worse story.

Another consideration when carrying is in crossing state lines. Not all states allow concealed carry, and not all states that permit concealed carry have reciprocity agreements in place with some or all of the other states that do. I live in Northern Virginia. I'm less than twenty-five miles from Washington, D.C., and Maryland, neither of which recognize my Virginia CCW permit. The Washington metro area is a maze of roads (thank you Pierre L'Enfant), often complicated by what seems, to those of us who live here, to be an unending stream of roadwork and closures. If you aren't familiar with the area, one wrong turn can put you on a road you can't escape from, and bingo, there you are in D.C. I've done it, luckily not with a gun in my possession, but I've done it, and then it can take twenty to thirty minutes to negotiate the labyrinth of one-way roads to get out.

Now, I'm not willing to test the law, but I have a feeling that proclaiming innocence by virtue of traffic isn't going to keep me out of jail if I make that wrong turn, get pulled over, and the police somehow discover I have a firearm concealed in the car. D.C. is the bigger of the two problems, as the District doesn't allow me (or just about anyone else) to have a firearm in the car. Maryland is a little more forgiving—if your firearm is unloaded, locked up, and inaccessible. Hard to do when you are on the interstate and suddenly see the "Welcome to Maryland" sign overhead.

To prevent such mishaps (and their resulting fines and possible jail time), the first thing you need to do is get familiar with your area and the laws of nearby states you're likely to cross into. Google is often a big help with this. My search there pulled up USACarry.com and PersonalDefenseWorld.com, for instance, both of which keep track of CCW laws for the various states. Check at least once a year, for your state and surrounding states, as the laws change and you may not hear about it.

What about suddenly remembering that you needed to stop by the post office? Or you have your gun on you and realize you need to pick up forms at the clerk of courts office? The answer to this and other similarly sticky situations is to make sure that you have a safe and secure means of storing firearms in your vehicle. GunVault (www.gunvault.com) makes a great little portable safe that has a steel cable integrated into it. This can be looped through a bracket in the trunk, the car seat frame, or other sturdy car part, and the safe gives you plenty of room for a gun, spare magazine, and, if you are going into a courthouse, your cell phone (since those are usually banned, as well).

GunVault is just one company that offers such safes. Regardless the one you choose, a word of caution: Use discretion in unholstering, securing, and re-holstering. You don't want to risk being accused of brandishing, nor do you want a passerby to see your firearm as you're storing it and mark your car as a target for a break-in. I have a hatchback, and

I've been known to sit in my trunk area with my gun side into the car so I can remove it from my holster without being seen. I've even sat in the back seat to secure it and stash it in a safe under a front seat.

Responsible gun owners know that we are safe, conscientious, and legal. However, there are a lot of people out there who believe no one should have a gun. Most of them can't come up with a cogent argument to support that, because their opinions are based on fear and a lack of understanding. Of course, these are often the same people who want you in front of them, with a gun, in an active shooter situation; logic isn't universal. Bottom line, the more discreet you are, the less likely you are to attract attention and run the risk of someone calling the police. I have a lot of respect for law enforcement, especially these days, but I prefer to deal with them when *I* want to, not because they're looking for me because someone reported me as having a firearm on the street.

4. Life Changes—So Should Your Gun Handling Skills

Different stages and events in our lives influence what we do and how we respond to certain stimuli. For example, you are probably familiar with the NRA's top three safety rules:

- Always keep the gun pointed in a safe direction.
- Always keep the gun unloaded until you are ready to use it.
- Always keep your finger off the trigger until ready to fire.

I have a fourth rule. Always wear shoes when you are handling your firearms.

How did I stumble upon this new safety rule? I had just cleaned my favorite Henry .22 lever-action rifle and was putting it back into the safe. It slipped, landed on my unshod foot, and *owww*!

My first thought, oddly enough, was of the rifle, worried that I had somehow damaged it. Then I saw a dark line on the top of my foot and thought that was odd, because I had just cleaned the whole gun, so how was there something dirty on the butt that I had missed? Ignoring the pain, I finished putting the gun away, secured the safe, and started to hobble toward the fridge for ice for my foot. That was when I realized the dark line was blood. Then the wave of pain hit, and I knew I was in trouble. Using an ACE bandage to secure a bag of frozen peas to the top of my foot, I quickly drove to the emergency room.

Now, imagine trying to explain what happened without using the word "gun." Jumping ahead, I got lucky. The gash wasn't too bad, they glued it together (lasted about twenty-four hours before it opened up again) and all those bones in the top of my foot were fine. My toe, however, was crushed. All three bones broken. To this day it is a little oddly shaped, and thanks to the destruction of the flexor tendon, it doesn't bend. But it did heal, no surgery, no pin.

This event, minor though it might be to some, led to a life event for me: the use of crutches. Impediments to one's ability

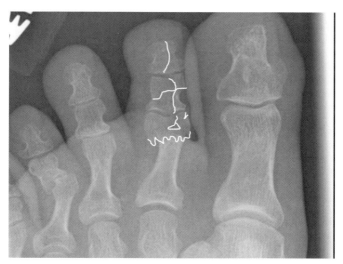

This is my X-ray. The highlights outline the fractures.

to walk can be very disconcerting, and the frustration and necessary adjustments can and will lead to lots of changes in how one does things.

For me, carrying a firearm on my body became a challenge. Normally, I carry on my strong-side hip. Could I do that with crutches? No! I had to switch to an appendix carry and then practice, a few inches in front of a wall in case I started to tip over, how to draw and extend my gun. I also practiced keeping my balance while using my crutch as a barrier or a club to push someone back, all without ending up on the ground myself.

There are many other life events that will cause you to make such adjustments to how you carry and train. I've talked with new moms who, as you might imagine, struggle to deal with a baby in their arms and a gun on their hip. With a new baby in their life, and often coupled with the physical changes that come to most with pregnancy and birth, new moms walk differently, plus they have strollers, car seats, diaper bags, and lots of other "stuff" to contend with. Mothers of toddlers have it even tougher, those terrible twos requiring constant, never-look-away attention.

According to the U.S. Census Bureau, in 2003, 14.1 percent of the population was sixty-five or older. The closer I get to sixty-five, the younger it seems. Nonetheless, many of us suffer wear-and-tear issues as we age. According to the Centers for Disease Control and Prevention (CDC) one in five, or 22.7 percent, of adults reported being diagnosed with arthritis, osteoarthritis being the most common form of the disease. Osteoarthritis is, essentially, the result of wear and tear on our various joints, the price many of us pay for being active when we were younger. Not everyone gets it, but, if you do, you will know it. The disease can impact knees and hips especially. That won't stop you from shooting, but it can make it harder to walk. I can hear some of you saying, "So what? That's just part of life." True, but do you realize those aging, slower-moving, and lame bodies to the practiced eye if a criminal are akin to a pride's lead lion looking at zebra with a broken leg? That's right, easy pickings.

Every stage of life brings its challenges. The keys to your safety include learning what you can do within the limitations at hand (crutches, pregnancy, arthritis), think about techniques that accommodate those limitations, and then practice to make the adjustment. Behind it all, though, is the most important thing of all, and that is to be *aware*. Aware that you can't access your gun from its normal holster position when you've got an arm in a cast. Aware that an injury to your strong hand means both a new holster position and lots more practice with weak-handed shooting. Aware that your infant learning to crawl and pull him- or herself up to a standing position probably means reassessing how and where you secure your firearms. Aware that up-to-date eyeglass prescriptions and hearing aids are boons to your awareness of things around you as you get older and these two senses decline in acuity.

The list goes on and on, of course. In later chapters I'll talk about techniques to carry during different activities, working around injuries, and other adjustments you'll likely need to make to how you carry as the years go by. But beyond the specifics, the point remains the one I talked about in the first chapter, and that is that carrying a firearm involves thinking about it—all the time! Think, prepare, adjust, and train. Rinse and repeat.

NSSF's Rules of Gun Safety

The National Shooting Sports Foundation (NSSF) is the trade association for the American firearms industry. Its mission is to promote, protect, and preserve hunting and the shooting sports. Though a trade association, the NSSF also serves an important role for consumers, providing a wealth of instructional and safety resources, including these Rules of Gun Safety (courtesy NSSF). For more information, visit www.nssf.org.

1. Always Keep the Muzzle Pointed in a Safe Direction—This is the most basic safety rule. If everyone handled a firearm so carefully that the muzzle never pointed at something they didn't intend to shoot, there would be virtually no firearms accidents. It's as simple as that, and it's up to you. Never point your gun at anything you do not intend to shoot. This is particularly important when loading or unloading a firearm. In the event of an accidental discharge, no injury can occur as long as the muzzle is pointing in a safe direction.

    A safe direction means a direction in which a bullet cannot possibly strike anyone, taking into account possible ricochets and the fact that bullets can penetrate walls and ceilings. The safe direction may be "up" on some occasions or "down" on others, but never at anyone or anything not intended as a target. Even when "dry firing" with an unloaded gun, you should never point the gun at an unsafe target. Make it a habit to know exactly where the muzzle of your gun is pointing at all times, and be sure that you are in control of the direction in which the muzzle is pointing, even if you fall or stumble. This is your responsibility, and only you can control it.

2. Firearms Should Be Unloaded When Not Actually in Use—Firearms should be loaded only when you are in the field or on the target range or shooting area, ready to shoot. When not in use, firearms and ammunition should be secured in a safe place, separate from each other. It is your responsibility to prevent children and unauthorized adults from gaining access to firearms or ammunition. Unload your gun as soon as you are finished. A loaded gun has no place in or near a car, truck, or building. Unload your gun immediately when you have finished shooting, well before you bring it into a car, camp, or home.

   Whenever you handle a firearm or hand it to someone, always open the action immediately and visually check the chamber, receiver and magazine to be certain they do not contain any ammunition. Always keep actions open when not in use. Never assume a gun is unloaded—check for yourself! This is considered a mark of an experienced gun handler!

   Never cross a fence, climb a tree, or perform any awkward action with a loaded gun. While in the field, there will be times when common sense and the basic rules of firearms safety will require you to unload your gun for maximum safety. Never pull or push a loaded firearm toward yourself or another person.

There is never any excuse to carry a loaded gun in a scabbard, a holster not being worn, or a gun case. When in doubt, unload your gun!

3. Don't Rely on Your Gun's "Safety"—Treat every gun as though it can fire at any time. The "safety" on any gun is a mechanical device that, like any such device, can become inoperable at the worst possible time. Besides, by mistake, the safety may be "off" when you think it is "on." The safety serves as a supplement to proper gun handling, but cannot possibly serve as a substitute for common sense. You should never handle a gun carelessly and assume that the gun won't fire just because the "safety is on."

4. Never touch the trigger on a firearm until you actually intend to shoot. Keep your fingers away from the trigger while loading or unloading. Never pull the trigger on any firearm with the safety on the "safe" position or anywhere in between "safe" and "fire." It is possible that the gun can fire at any time, or even later when you release the safety, without you ever having to touch the trigger again. Never place the safety in between positions, since half-safe is unsafe. Keep the safety "on" until you are absolutely ready to fire.

Regardless of the position of the safety, any blow or jar strong enough to actuate the firing mechanism of a gun can cause it to fire. This can happen even if the trigger is not touched, such as when a gun is dropped.

Never rest a loaded gun against any object, because there is always the possibility that it will be jarred or slide from its position and fall with sufficient force to discharge. The only time you can be absolutely certain that a gun cannot fire is when the action is open and it is completely empty. Again, never rely on your gun's safety. You and the safe gun handling procedures you have learned are your gun's primary safeties.

5. Be Sure of Your Target and What's Beyond It—No one can call a shot back. Once a gun fires, you have given up all control over where the shot will go or what it will strike. Don't shoot unless you know exactly what your shot is going to strike. Be sure that your bullet will not injure anyone or anything beyond your target. Firing at a movement or a noise without being absolutely certain of what you are shooting at constitutes disregard for the safety of others. No target is so important that you cannot take the time before you pull the trigger to be absolutely certain of your target and where your shot will stop.

6. Be aware that even a .22 Short bullet can travel more than 1¼ miles and a high-velocity cartridge, such as a .30-06, can send its bullet more than three miles. Shotgun pellets can travel 500 yards, and shotgun slugs have a range of more than a half-mile. You should keep in mind how far a bullet will travel if it misses your intended target or ricochets in another direction.

7. Use Correct Ammunition—You must assume the serious responsibility of using only the correct ammunition for your firearm. Read and heed all warnings, including those that appear in the gun's instruction manual and on the ammunition boxes.

8. Using improper or incorrect ammunition can destroy a gun and cause serious personal injury. It only takes one cartridge of improper caliber or gauge to wreck

your gun, and only a second to check each one as you load it. Be absolutely certain that the ammunition you are using matches the specifications that are contained within the gun's instruction manual and the manufacturer's markings on the firearm.

Firearms are designed, manufactured, and proof tested to standards based upon those of factory loaded ammunition. Handloaded or reloaded ammunition deviating from pressures generated by factory loads or from component recommendations specified in reputable handloading manuals can be dangerous and can cause severe damage to guns and serious injury to the shooter. Do not use improper reloads or ammunition made of unknown components.

Ammunition that has become very wet or has been submerged in water should be discarded in a safe manner. Do not spray oil or solvents on ammunition or place ammunition in excessively lubricated firearms. Poor ignition, unsatisfactory performance, or damage to your firearm and harm to yourself or others could result from using such ammunition.

Form the habit of examining every cartridge you put into your gun. Never use damaged or substandard ammunition; the money you save is not worth the risk of possible injury or a ruined gun.

9. If Your Gun Fails to Fire When the Trigger is Pulled, Handle with Care!— Occasionally, a cartridge may not fire when the trigger is pulled. If this occurs, keep the muzzle pointed in a safe direction. Keep your face away from the breech. Then, carefully open the action,

unload the firearm and dispose of the cartridge in a safe way.

Any time there is a cartridge in the chamber, your gun is loaded and ready to fire, even if you've tried to shoot and it did not go off. It could go off at any time, so you must always remember Rule No. 1 and watch that muzzle!

Discharging firearms in poorly ventilated areas, cleaning firearms, or handling ammunition may result in exposure to lead and other substances known to cause birth defects, reproductive harm, and other serious physical injury. Have adequate ventilation at all times. Wash hands thoroughly after exposure.

10. Always Wear Eye and Ear Protection When Shooting— All shooters should wear protective shooting glasses and some form of hearing protectors while shooting. Exposure to shooting noise can damage hearing, and adequate vision protection is essential. Shooting glasses guard against twigs, falling shot, clay target chips, and the rare ruptured case or firearm malfunction. Wearing eye protection when disassembling and cleaning any gun will also help prevent the possibility of springs, spring tension parts, solvents, or other agents from contacting your eyes. There is a wide variety of eye and ear protectors available. No target shooter, plinker, or hunter should ever be without them.

11. Most rules of shooting safety are intended to protect you and others around you, but this rule is for your protection alone. Furthermore, having your hearing and eyes protected will make your shooting easier and will help improve your enjoyment of the shooting sports.

12. Be Sure the Barrel is Cleared of Obstruction before Shooting—Before you load your firearm, open the action and be certain that no ammunition is in the chamber or magazine. Be sure the barrel is clear of any obstruction. Even a small bit of mud, snow, excess lubricating oil, or grease in the bore can cause dangerously increased pressures, causing the barrel to bulge or even burst on firing, which can cause injury to the shooter and bystanders. Make it a habit to clean the bore and check for obstructions with a cleaning rod immediately before you shoot it. If the noise or recoil on firing seems weak or doesn't seem quite "right," cease firing immediately and be sure to check that no obstruction or projectile has become lodged in the barrel.

    Placing a smaller gauge or caliber cartridge into a gun (such as a 20-gauge shell in a 12-gauge shotgun) can result in the smaller cartridge falling into the barrel and acting as a bore obstruction when a cartridge of proper size is fired. This can cause a burst barrel or worse. This is really a case where "haste makes waste." You can easily avoid this type of accident by paying close attention to each cartridge you insert into your firearm.

13. Don't Alter Your Guns, And Have Guns Serviced Regularly—Firearms are complicated mechanisms that are designed by experts to function properly in their original condition. Any alteration or change made to a firearm after manufacture can make the gun dangerous and will usually void any factory warranties. Do not jeopardize your safety or the safety of others by altering the trigger, safety, or other mechanism of any firearm or allowing unqualified persons to repair or modify a gun. You'll usually ruin an expensive gun. Don't do it!

Your gun is a mechanical device that will not last forever and is subject to wear. As such, it requires periodic inspection, adjustment, and service. Check with the manufacturer of your firearm for recommended servicing.

14. Learn the Mechanical and Handling Characteristics of the Firearm You Are Using—Not all firearms are the same. The method of carrying and handling firearms varies in accordance with the mechanical characteristics of each gun. Since guns can be so different, never handle any firearm without first having thoroughly familiarized yourself with the particular type of firearm you are using, the safe gun handling rules for loading, unloading, carrying, and handling that firearm, and the rules of safe gun handling in general.

For example, many handgun manufacturers recommend that their handguns always be carried with the hammer down on an empty chamber. This is particularly true for older single-action revolvers, but applies equally to some double-action revolvers or semiautomatic pistols. You should always read and refer to the instruction manual you received with your gun, or, if you have misplaced the manual, simply contact the manufacturer for a free copy.

Having a gun in your possession is a full-time job. You cannot guess; you cannot forget. You must know how to use, handle, and store your firearm safely. Do not use any firearm without having a complete understanding of its particular characteristics and safe use. There is no such thing as a foolproof gun.

5. Rethinking Situational Awareness

Situational Awareness is the ability to identify, process, and comprehend the critical elements of information about what is happening to the team with regards to the mission. More simply, it's knowing what is going on around you.

—U.S. Coast Guard Team Coordination Training
Student Guide 8/98

Situational awareness is a critical component of carrying a firearm for self-defense (or, really, any defense). As the Coast Guard training manual says, it's about *knowing what's going on around you.*

You probably can recall hearing the occasional story of a pedestrian here and there getting hit by a car because they were wearing iPhone headphones or were text messaging as they stepped into the street. That's a lack of situational awareness. The woman who walks blindly to her car in the dark parking garage, briefcase and purse slung over one arm and chatting away on her cell with the other, who gets an arm clamped around her mouth and a knife to her throat? Yup, she lacked situational awareness, too.

A lack of situational awareness can result in a multitude of, well, injuries. Were you trying to get your screaming child to settle down in the back seat and missed your exit? Pretty minor. Your failure to notice a shady-looking character on the other side of the street abruptly crossing the pavement and following you? That could result in something far worse.

Recently, several events came together in a synergistic way that caused me to rethink my situational awareness. One of these events occurred when interviewing Melody Lauer of Central Iowa Defensive Training. In that interview, we discussed her teaching technique of focusing on threat assessment rather than situational awareness.

Many instructors talk about situational awareness. The late Jeff Cooper, a former Marine and one of America's premier combat instructors, even developed what came to be known as Cooper's Color Code to describe various levels of situational awareness, and that code has been used in the core curriculum of self-defense instructors, police, and military the world over (see sidebar). But, discussions on situational awareness are too often approached in a way that leaves the student thinking they need to be looking everywhere at once and processing everything. Who can deal with that much sensory input? Not me! I don't try, either. Like Melody, when I'm scanning my surroundings, I am also assessing the people and situations I see to gauge any risk that might be associated with them.

In the following paragraphs, I will describe the model I developed to replace my older situational awareness training module. I still believe in situational awareness, but I think there's a more approachable level to it than some of the older models out there permit.

Jeff Cooper's Awareness Color Code

Hang around guns and gun people long enough and you'll eventually hear the name Jeff Cooper. Born in 1920, John Dean "Jeff" Cooper joined the Marines in 1941, serving in the Pacific Theater during the WWII, then later joining the US efforts in the Korean War. Cooper was a well-educated man, and, in addition to his military career, taught high school and community college classes. In the mid-1970s, he founded the American Pistol Institute in Pauldon, Arizona. Now known as the famed Gunsite Academy, the shooting facility is one of Cooper's most lasting legacies.

Part of that legacy lies in Cooper's development of the Modern Pistol Technique, but in self-defense circles, he's probably best known for his teachings on the "combat mindset" and the development of his "color code."

Cooper's color code of awareness and subsequent preparedness is best simplified as follows:

1. White—You are unaware and unprepared to deal with an attack.
2. Yellow—You're alert, but relaxed. No threat is present, but you should be watching your "six," that blind spot behind you. According to Cooper, you should always be at yellow if you're in unfamiliar surroundings or amongst people you don't know.

3. Orange—Something isn't quite right, and it has attracted your attention. You will study to assess the threat with the recognition that you might have to shoot. "If such and such happens, I will do this to stop it."
4. Red—Now you're in an actual fight and in lethal mode.

Cooper's teachings continue to hold a tremendous amount of sway with military, law enforcement, and civilian self-defense practitioners. His legacy Gunsite Academy is one of the most popular destinations for people of all walks looking to improve their defensive skills, and one of the most respected teaching facilities in the country. He authored a number of books on self-defense and riflecraft while he was alive, and they, as well as Gunsite (www.gunsite.com), are certainly worth exploring.

RPA—Recognize, Prepare, and Act

The first step in using the RPA system I developed is to "recognize" a potential threat. This entails being aware of your surroundings, taking time to scan with your eyes and with your gut, and quickly ranking what you see so that you can focus on the most likely threat or threats. This ranking can, and likely will, change as you move from a place of relative security, such as a store or your home neighborhood, into a place of significant risk, such as a covered parking lot or a section of town notorious for its daytime crime. When you approach those riskier places, keep your senses tuned to identify those people or situations that might pose the highest risk to you.

Now, that doesn't mean you need to spend time trying to memorize every detail or identify the colors of all the cars. Instead, see who is within your "safety circle" (see the sidebar), who is coming close, who is exiting. If you are in a parking lot, take note of any oversized vehicle that could hide someone and is parked next to yours. Do you see anyone acting in a way that feels weird or wrong? Does someone seem to be paying too much attention to you? Is someone moving directly toward you with their hands in their pockets while they are glancing side to side as if checking to see who else might be around? Do you see a young mom with several children, juggling packages on the way to her car? An elderly couple shuffling toward you slowly and holding hands? A teenage boy in a hoodie with jeans down around his hips? A man in a suit talking into a Bluetooth device? Three older teens gathered close together and handling "something" between them, each taking turns keeping watch outside their circle?

Taking each of those possibilities, it probably seems easy to assign "likely" or "unlikely" to each of them, regarding the threat level you perceive they might have. And, in fact, the ease with which you do that should tell you something. You see, you can assign a threat value with very little information, in less than a second, and *without* overwhelming yourself.

Also know that assigning risk, quickly and on the fly as you go, doesn't mean you stop being aware of other people and situations around you. Circumstances change, and you need to recognize those changes and reassess their risk values. However, these quick judgments can help you focus on the *most* likely threats wherever you are, and that gives you a chance to prepare.

The Tueller Drill

For the better part of three decades, maybe more, law enforcement across the country has trained their officers on the Tueller Drill. Succinctly put, a person wielding a knife just twenty-one feet away can be on you in a physical attack before you can recognize that things are about to go south, draw your firearm, and fire it in self-protection. So hardwired is the Tueller Drill into the core curriculum of law enforcement and self-defense instructors everywhere that, if you take the time to participate in a class of this kind, you'll likely hear it talked about. I incorporated the Tueller Drill into the "safety circle" discussion, i.e., twenty-one feet around you in any direction is the minimum you'll need if you have to draw your gun from its holster and fire a shot at an imminent and deadly threat.

In recent years, the Tueller Drill has been examined from many angles. Much of the discussion pertains to officer-justified shootings and is not relative to this book. What is germane to this book is that the twenty-one feet of distance long attested to as being the minimum required for one to recognize an edged-weapon threat and react with a drawn and fired firearm is now considered by many to be too close.

What does that mean for you? Well, first it means you should have a really good idea of what twenty-one feet from you looks like. Humans are notoriously bad at judging distance, even something as relatively short as twenty-one feet. So go out to your back yard and measure twenty-one feet from a tree or the kids' swing set. Go to the park and measure twenty-one feet from the park bench by the pond or the drinking fountain by the dog run area (and ignore the people who give you a sideways look). Do this in different places until you get pretty good at figuring out what twenty-one feet looks like. Now extend that range to thirty feet. That thirty-foot mark is what many in law enforcement are looking at as the potential new standard distance for a trained officer (emphasis on trained) to recognize an imminent edged-weapons attack, draw their gun, and get off a shot or two.

Do you want to extend that distance farther? Maybe. Depends on your level of training and how well you've honed your RPA skills. How much farther, though, has a limit. A guy running from 100 feet away and in your direction may be a threat or he may not be. You won't recognize whether he's a threat until he gets closer (though it would be a smart thing to get your hand on your gun's grip and prepare for action). Sure, it may be a madman coming for you. But what if it's a trim and lithe girl with a short haircut and she just took that knife from *her* attacker and is running away from *him?* You can't tell from 100 feet away, all you can do is prepare to respond if that person is realized to be an attacker coming for *you*. As for longer distances, well, you better be running for cover your-self, because there's likely time for you to initiate some action other than drawing and firing a gun.

Of course, the dynamics of distance and defense change if gunfire is coming from the threat to you. If you're being fired upon, or have reason to believe you're going to be (a thug is pointing his gun in your direction and yelling "I'm gonna shoot you!") from a close distance, well, then I hope you were aware of your surroundings, had possible cover staked out, and had your gun drawn to rcturn fire. What about fifty, 100, or more yards? It's often hard to identify where a shot is coming from at such distances, especially if the gunman is concealed or the venue is crowded. Your best bet is to seek immediate cover while preparing to defend yourself should the attack become closer to and directed at you.

The Safety Circle is still an incredibly useful tool to have in your arsenal of knowledge, and not just for defense against an edged weapon attack. The point is to be *aware* and cognizant of the potential danger closest to you, and within a distance that allows you time to react appropriately.

The second part of RPA is to "prepare." Prepare means that you are considering "what ifs." What if that guy who crossed the street and changed directions is quite obviously following you? Are you looking around at your surroundings and assessing which places my provide sanctuary or help? Are you close enough to your car to get into it, lock the doors, and ready your firearm? Now let's say it was an elderly couple who crossed the street and were coming towards you? Do you need to prepare to deal with them? Probably not, except maybe a polite smile. Assessing and what-iffing in this quick manner lets your brain think about what to do if the potential threat becomes a real threat and, in doing so, prepares you to act.

"Acting," of course, is the final step in RPA. Acting simply means taking whatever action you can to avoid (always a good first choice), or respond (when there isn't another choice), to a threat. What kind of action will be required? Any kind. It may mean turning around and going back into the store you just came out of. Maybe you cross the street and enter a crowded restaurant, or perhaps you pick up your pace and get in your car, locking the doors and leaving immediately. It could also mean bracing for a direct confrontation and doing what you need to, within your skill level and using what tools you have available, to survive.

The diagram above is constructed to show how all the aspects of a confrontation are inter-related, and also demon-strate that you can jump between those aspects quickly. Bad situations are "dynamic," meaning they are characterized by constant change—and if the situation's a bad

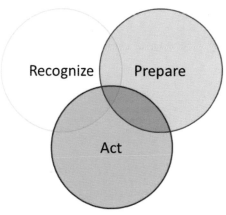

The RPA System: Notice how the components intersect and overlap.

one, those changes tend to happen very fast. *You* need to be dynamic and faster to come out of it all in one piece.

The concept of RPA is a simple one, but also one that's very manageable. It does require that you are aware. Previously I have written about the "safety circle," that twenty-one feet of space around you that shouldn't be violated without your awareness (see sidebar). RPA doesn't change that. However, if you are using RPA correctly, you are aware of people and potential threats before they breach your circle. This awareness gives you time to plan and react in a manner that, hopefully, keeps you safe.

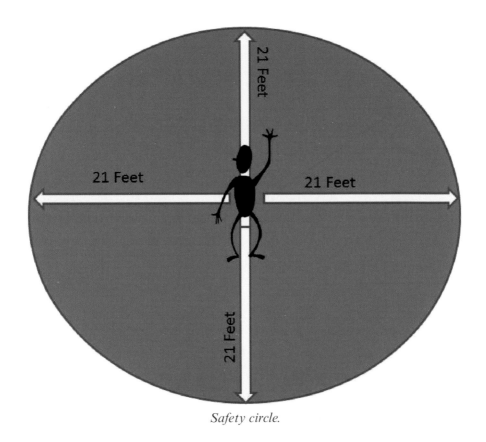

Safety circle.

Improving RPA with Reflections

One tool that provides significant support for RPA is the use of reflective surfaces. Mirrors, car windows, glass storefronts—all can expand your field of vision. Being able to see behind you and to the side, those things out of your immediate peripheral vision, can buy you time to react.

Once on a trip to Las Vegas with my significant other, we were walking down the sidewalk in front of a strip mall. A man pulled into the parking lot separating the walk from the mall front. He proceeded to walk along in front of the stores in the opposite direction we were walking, but then turned and gradually accelerated until he was pacing us, about twenty feet away. My partner and I took turns making eye contact, letting him know we were aware of him. Eventually he turned, went back to his car, and drove away.

Do I have any doubt we were being sized up? None. Do I believe that our level of awareness was enough to convince him we were not going to be caught by surprise? Absolutely. Criminals want the compliant, unaware, easy target. Don't give it to them.

Part II
Self-Defense Tactics for Everyday Life

6. Everyone Goes to the Mall

Everyone. That's why I'm making the discussion of defending yourself while visiting such shopping centers its own chapter. There are special considerations based on your physical condition that will be addressed elsewhere, but let's start with the premise that leaving a relatively safe environment (the inside of a mall, shopping center, or other store), to enter an area of significantly higher risk (such as a parking lot or a side street to get back to your car), is a multi-stage process.

Before You Leave

You've finished shopping, bags are in hand, and you're about to leave for your car. Now is the time to take inventory: Do you have your keys out? Do you have everyone and everything you went in with, your purse, sunglasses, and other shopping bags? Is your vision unobstructed by all the packages you are juggling? Is your firearm still accessible? If these all get a "Yes," then okay, take a deep breath and step outside.

Scan the Area

As soon as you step outside—or, even better, before you step outside, if you can get a good view through storefront windows—scan the immediate area around the exit. Does anyone seem out of place or menacing? If yes, go back in the store and ask a security guard to walk you to your car. Most won't have any problem with that, but they don't advertise that they will do this for you. If no security guard is around, then have a couple store managers escort you.

Everything look good at the exit point? Move on to scanning that path to your car and see who is in your path or adjacent to it. Nothing threatening? What vehicles are parked next to yours? If it's, say, a large van or SUV, especially one that blocks your view of others (because then others also likely can't see you), you may want to enter your car from the other side. Trust your instincts.

Don't Dawdle

Now walk as briskly and purposefully as you can to your car, keeping note of who's around you as you go. Once you get to your car, unlock only the doors you need to. Remember, if you're pushing a shopping cart, it's possible to use it as a barrier while you load bags into your car—but you have to look up from what you're doing and check around you every few seconds.

Small children can complicate things. Put packages in the car before the kids, as a casual mugger is more likely to go after the loot than the kids. Once the packages are stowed, you are a lesser target. Next, open only one door. One kid needs to go in first, one at time while leaving the other doors locked, and secure that child before repeating for other children and other doors. You, of course, come last. When it's time, unlock your door only, get in, and relock the vehicle all the way around. The goal is to safely stow your cargo and people while leaving as few openings as possible to outsiders.

Handy Tools

If you knew you wouldn't be leaving your shopping area until night had fallen and had planned ahead for that, then you parked under a light. Do not park next to large vehicles or in dark corners if you can help it; if you're shopping in areas you regularly go, you should know which areas stay bright and which ones do not. Also, since darkness arrives at various times depending on the season, be prepared for some parking areas to be dark when you've finished shopping and park elsewhere, beforehand, when possible.

Things happen. You run into a friend while you're shopping, you stayed later than you'd intended, and now it's dark as you're about to leave. A small flashlight can really come in handy in cases like this, as well as when you do know you won't return to your car until dark. A flashlight is also good for the unexpected. I once got off the subway and entered the parking garage, only to discover all the lights were out. I was the only one in the mass of people standing at the entrance to the garage who could find their car—because I had a flashlight. You never know. I keep a small one on my keychain just for such things. Shining a little light can be handy.

I also keep a personal alarm hanging on my purse. I make it a habit to carry my handbag with the alarm to the front and accessible. It isn't really "defensive," but it makes a lot of noise and can attract a lot of attention. Plus, it isn't really noticeable because it hangs with charms on a clip that easily changes from one bag to another.

Trust Your Intuition

If it feels wrong, take action. Go back to the store you came out of or find another business that's open, nearby, and active. Are you closer to your car? Can you get in and lock the doors? Once inside, if someone approaches before you get the car started and moving, you can lay on the horn. Predators like easy prey. Awareness, noise, and light are all things they would rather avoid.

Personal alarm.

Don't suppress your initial response to something that seems weird or out of place. In his book *The Gift of Fear,* Gavin de Becker addresses trusting that discomfort. Your senses are telling you something. Listen to them, and don't worry about someone thinking you are foolish. If something doesn't feel right, it probably isn't, even if you don't know exactly what it is that's bothering you, and it's better to have taken action and stayed safe even if something wasn't a threat than it is to keep going and do nothing to prevent or prepare for an attack to happen.

The Kid Equation

Few things are as scary as a confrontation that occurs when you have kids with you. Remember that most muggers are more interested in quick cash than they are in hurting a child. That's the good news, because being attacked while you have children in your immediate care changes the intensity of the response from bystanders and police. Think about it. You might not respond or interfere with a simple mugging of a lone adult, but if a child is screaming, how many of us could stand by? That said, Melody Lauer, referenced earlier, has developed training specific to being armed and having your children with you.

Melody advocates learning to get your little ones into their car seats without having to look at what you're doing. Why? Because, if you do not have your head down fumbling for buckles, you can be scanning the area for potential threats. Putting the babies in the car can leave you vulnerable if you are too task focused. I know, there are lots of straps and buckles, not to mention the often struggling, screaming toddler, but, with practice, you should be able to get everyone buckled in while keeping your eyes on the environment outside the car and over your shoulder. Don't believe me? Do you need to look at the buttons on your shirt to fasten them? Of course not, you know how to do that without looking, thanks to years and years of practice.

Keep in mind that as small children develop fine motor skills, they can actually help streamline the process of strapping themselves into a car. My daughter was very cooperative about getting in her car seat as a small child. She had never known any other way, and my partner and I had made it a game, calling it "Be Safe." Older toddlers who understand the buckles can snap them together and then you can feel and/or quickly look to make sure they got it right, allowing you to remain focused on what's going on around you.

The next-to-worst-case scenario when leaving any shopping area is that you have become targeted. If you believe this is happening and reentering the store or other business isn't an option, you're going to need to move fast, hustling the kids into the car and locking the doors, luring the attacker away from *them*. If the situation is truly urgent, you can quickly place children on the vehicle seat or floor, then jump in and drive to a safer location where you can then buckle them in.

In the most dangerous of situations, you may have to step away from the children in your care, and leave them exposed, in order to deal with a threat. This sounds harsh, but, again, a mugger is more likely interested in you than the kids. If you can put a little distance between the attack and the children, they are likely to be safer, and you are free to deal with the situation. Yes, it is counter-intuitive for most parents to separate themselves from their children, but doing so can make a lot of sense. The trick, really, is to balance the need to respond in the way with which you are most comfortable against tactics that provide the best chance of safety for all involved.

Keys in Your Hand

At the beginning of this chapter, one of the things I advised you to do before leaving a store was to have your car keys in hand. There are a couple reasons for this.

The most obvious is that if you have a potential threat in close proximity to you, you're able to get in your car—and with only the driver's door unlocked if it's just you and you hit your remote button just once— much faster than if you have to go digging in your purse for your keys.

That digging around in your purse is a second reason to have your keys in hand before you leave a store. As you head to your car, you're burdened with packages and maybe children, plus your cell phone and handbag—and, if you're a mom, it's likely a big handbag.

Do this: go dig in your purse right now for your keys. How long did it take you to find them? How long did it take you to distinguish your keys from your wallet and snack bars and water bottle and hairbrush and mascara and lipstick tubes? A couple seconds? Thirty? Did you have to pull all that stuff out of your handbag and then look inside before you recovered your keys?

Did someone sneak up behind you while you were doing that at your car door?

Keys in your hand serve another purpose besides expediency and allowing you to stay cognizant of what's going on around you. Keys can also serve as a weapon. Hold onto your keychain or one big key and smash the rest into an attacker's face. Have one of those shorter six-inch Kubatons as your key chain? Perfect. Now you can swing, with great force, your keys into someone's face, and you can use the Kubaton (or that flashlight in your other hand) to stab them in the throat or eyes. While that may not fend off every attacker, such actions may just give you enough time to run away or get in your car and speed off.

7. Intermediate Measures

I f the gun is a last resort, and you've been vigilant and find yourself in a potentially dangerous situation, do you know about, have available, and have practiced with intermediate measures? Let's explore some of the most common and easily used tools that are options that can come before the gun.

Pepper Spray

This stuff is nasty, but not all pepper sprays are created equal, and some people are able to develop a level of immunity to some sprays. I encourage you to look for SabreRed, which is available from the company's website (www.sabrered.com), through Amazon.com, and from many retailers. SabreRed comes in multiple configurations that make the canisters easy to carry no matter your circumstance or activity. Some dispensers also contain a UV dye that marks the person sprayed for several days, making them more easily identifiable (as if the red mask of irritated skin wasn't enough).

Pepper spray can be very effective, but using it properly takes practice. (Also, do check your local laws, as some areas require pepper spray to be registered, or it may be restricted based on age.) For instance, you should practice getting comfortable flipping the trigger off the safe position quickly, and you should know how to orient the canister to activate the spray.

Spray in short, three- to five-second bursts, sweeping back and forth across the eyebrows. This will cause the spray to run down into the eyes, even if the person is wearing glasses. You can have your other hand up defensively, but keep it behind the canister to avoid splashing your own hand. Once you spray, *move!* If someone is coming at you,

Pepper spray.

Using pepper spray.

their momentum will probably keep them coming toward you, and if you are where they last saw you, you may still get caught.

Tactical Flashlight

These aren't your mama's flashlights. Tactical flashlights, such as those from 5.11 Tactical (www.511tactical.com), Fenix (www.fenixlighting.com), and others, are available from most gun shops, outdoor stores, and Amazon.com. You will find them to be little more expensive than the plastic models you can get at the hardware store or Wal-Mart, but a good one is worth every penny. They are heavy, rugged, and extremely bright. A bonus is that many have a bezel that is toothed, enabling you to turn one into an effective striking tool (much like the keys I talked about in the last chapter). You can also flash a light into someone's eyes, temporarily interrupting their night vision and potentially giving you time to run away. In an attack situation, move immediately after you flash your opponent in their eyes. Just as it is with pepper spray, don't be standing in the last place they saw you when their vision clears up.

Tactical flashlights.

Tasers

Contrary to common language, tasers are not stun guns. A taser shoots prongs from a firearm-like device, those prongs attached to the device by wires through which an electrical charge is transmitted. The laws regarding the use of tasers by those not credentialed law enforcement personnel vary from state to state.

If you are permitted to own and use one of these tools, know that a taser is most effective if the person is not wearing a heavy outer garment, as the prongs need to penetrate the clothing and stick into skin. Also, you will need to practice with them (on a pile of clothing, a paper target—*not* a human), and now you can do that with models that can be "reloaded."

To paraphrase the great Muhammad Ali: "Shoots like a butterfly but stings like a bee."

Stun Guns

A stun gun is a handheld device that has prongs at its head and which transmit an electrical jolt between the prongs through a conductor, such as a person. They also make a very distinctive and scary snap-crackle sound.

Of course, you should never count on the sound to scare off someone. A bigger problem with a stun gun, though, is that these must be pressed into the attacker, so you will be in very close contact with an attacker to use one (and that's the advantage of the taser, because the long wires allow the person firing the device to maintain some distance between them and their aggressor). You also need to prolong that contact, and that can be a problem in a physical struggle.

A quick, half-second burst from a stun gun will hurt, but likely not deter, someone. Having accidently zapped myself, I can attest that it hurt, but it was not incapacitating (and, no, I won't tell you how I did it). You need a consistent two to three seconds of contact to really slow down someone. That's a long time, especially since your opponent isn't likely to be compliant and idle while you're trying to inflict some pain on him. Also, stun guns are more effective near bony areas that have large nerve bundles, such as a hip or shoulder.

A close-quarters physical struggle increases the possibility that any defensive tool you have can be taken and turned against you. To minimize your risk with a stun gun, choose a model that has a wrist strap and safety pin configuration so that, if the weapon is taken from you, the pin is pulled at the same time, disabling the device.

Stun gun.

Just as with tasers, local laws can vary regarding possession of stun guns. Before you invest and carry, be sure you know what the laws are in your area.

Collapsible Batons

These are known as flick-and-strike weapons. The "flick" part means you'll need to have a firm grasp on the baton handle and then flick it hard, as if you were bringing a ruler down on a table to get your kids' attention, in order to extend the baton to its full length and lock that length in place. The brand name Kubaton, as I mentioned in the Chapter 6 sidebar on keys, is one type of these, the ASP brand is another.

Collapsible batons are, like other tools I've talked about, for use in close-quarters attack situations, i.e., you're going to be grappling with someone or have them otherwise very close to you. They take practice to use effectively, something best taught by an instructor proficient in hand-to-hand combat

Collapsible batons are for use in close-quarter attack situations.

techniques. As it is with the other tools in this chapter, collapsible batons are not legal in all states.

Personal Alarms

This is, essentially, a noisemaker, and they are great for anyone
from teenagers to octogenarians. They can clip on a belt, bag,
or purse. Most have a pin connection so that, when you pull
on the alarm, it disconnects, activating the noise. They are
loud. The most effective way to use one is to pull that pin and
toss it away, so that someone else can't easily reinsert the pin
and shut off the device.

Personal alarms are
inexpensive and can attract
a lot of attention from
bystanders. My preference
is one made by SabreRed.
It has good battery life and is sleek and easy to use.

SabreRed personal alarm.

Baseball Bats and Golf Clubs

We can't leave out the trusty baseball bat or golf club when talking about self-defense tools. Slipped under the bed or standing in a corner, either of these can quickly be deployed to push off an attacker or used as a club during a physical attack. If you get into a wrestling match for control of the bat, you will have the advantage if you are holding it by the handle. If an attacker gets his hands on the bat at the same time, you can use a quick thrust-forward/jerk-back movement to break their grip, or you can roll the bat to the outside, breaking their grip and allowing you to bring it back and then forward for a quick strike.

Baseball bat.

All intermediate measures and tools are intended to buy you time to transition to your firearm, escape, or cause the attacker to realize you are not a compliant victim and move on. No matter what you decide to have as an intermediate measure option, you must practice with it, and it must be accessible when you need it. A pepper spray canister in the bottom of a purse doesn't do you any good at all.

8. Driving With a Defensive Mindset

J ust because you're tucked neatly in your car and driving around familiar roads doesn't mean your need for RPA or situational awareness disappears. Let's talk about why paying attention to more than the everyday road distractions can keep you out of trouble, and some of the things you can do behind the wheel if you suspect trouble is about to happen to you.

Mirror, Mirror

Whether you're driving down familiar neighborhood roads, zooming down highways, or tapping your steering wheel with frustration while stuck in standstill traffic, you should be glancing around you and using your mirrors to keep an eye on what's going on around you. Now, you should, of course, be doing this anyway, to keep an eye on other drivers and traffic movement as part of being an experienced and safe driver—but I know plenty of people who glance at their side or rearview mirrors only when they need to change lanes or back out of a parking spot.

We've all heard stories of women who have been followed home after leaving an empty parking lot long after the office closed for everyone else, even more so those often semi-inebriated women who are followed home from bars or parties—and you don't ever hear about those stories ending with a Jehovah's Witness knocking on the door asking if they've been saved.

Your mirrors are crucial not only to staying safe as a driver, but also to picking up on things weird and out of place. Is someone coming down the adjacent lane far faster than anyone else? Are other vehicles getting out of its way? Does a car pull in suddenly behind you? Does it appear to be trying to force you into an accident or off the road, especially if you're in a relatively uncongested area where there's no one to see what's about to happen? What if you're just waiting with a few other vehicles for the light to change? That could be a time ripe for a carjacking, but if you're not watching your mirrors to spot someone coming up to your car in a shady manner, how do you prepare to pull out of line and get away?

What do you do when something like that happens, where do you go?

Answering those last two questions can depend a lot on where you are and the others surrounding you. It can also depend on your cell phone coverage—hard to call for help with one bar out of five on the reception reading. Still, there are certain things you can do to avoid being victimized if you suspect you're going to be forced out of your car.

The first and most obvious would be to keep driving until you come across a patrol car, arrive at a crowded, active place with lots of other people, or can get to a police station. Do *not* drive home—someone intent on doing you harm may see a well-lit house and other cars in the driveway and decide then is not the time, but now he knows where you live and he can come back at his leisure.

Use your mirrors every time you drive to keep tabs on the cars around you. Is one making a turn or switching lanes every time you do? Is it always just a car or two behind you? If you suspect you're being followed, make an unexpected turn, maybe even without your turn signal on, and see if the car continues behind you. Do this, just as you would if you thought you were being forced into an accident or off the road, and make your turns in busy, active neighborhoods or town sections. Still following you? Try to get to a police station or hospital, someplace where there's likely to be law enforcement—and don't be polite about parking in the visitors' lot. Pull right up to the brightly lit emergency entrance and blow your car horn for all its worth. Better to explain why you're parked "illegally" than get mugged in the parking lot.

Give Yourself Space

Another key to defensive driving is to leave space between you and the car in front of you, especially at a traffic light. If you can't see the tires of the car in front of you, you are too close and have no chance of maneuvering if, say, a carjacker comes up on you suddenly. In crowded urban areas, leaving this kind of space between cars can be a challenge, with pushy, anxious drivers honking and trying to cut into the gap. Be firm—that space adds security to *your* space, and yours is the only one that counts.

There's another reason to leave space. It's a tactic of some thieves, carjackers, and other nefarious sorts to rear-end you and push you into the car in front of you, which will contain one of their partners in crime. You'll get out, they'll get out, and then things are likely not going to end well. Avoid the potential for getting caught up in this kind of setup by leaving enough space between you and the next car.

Ideally, you want to leave enough space so that you could potentially pull out of your lane and get away from a situation if you needed to (provided the traffic patterns could allow for that, which, of course, isn't possible on many city streets, narrow back roads and the like). But, even if you are blocked in on both sides, if you were rear-ended, you would have a better chance of not being pushed into the car in front of you when providing yourself with enough space between you and the car in front of you, and that could spoil a planned carjacking, robbery, or even those insurance scam setups that use this tactic.

Dash Cams

Once available only to law enforcement, dashboard cameras ("dash cams," for short) have hit the mass consumer market. They are available in a variety of price points and options from basic models that suction-cup to your dash and provide some sort of minimal recording time, on up to high-end, super fancy versions that get hardwired to your car's electrical system and have features like GPS, traffic camera alerts, and night recording built in, among other upgrades.

Mine is a pretty basic model I bought on Amazon.com. It records in a ten-minute loop on a micro card, and the unit itself powers up by plugging it into the lighter outlet.

Why would I want a dash cam? For one, I live in a densely populated area, and I have a significant commute to work. I spend a lot of time in traffic, and there are some crazy drivers out there. But a dash cam can be useful for more than just recording vehicle contact accidents.

Imagine being targeted in a road rage incident. A dash cam recording may prove you were the victim, not the initiator. It could also help prove your innocence in an accident where the other person blames you. How about a carjacking attempt where you are forced to defend yourself? The action may be caught, at least partially, on camera, giving proof to your side of the story and even helping to identify the carjacker if they flee the scene.

Beyond situations like that, there are all kinds of drivers doing all kinds of mindless things. Ever see someone at a light

Can you see the tires of the car in front of you? If not, you have no room to maneuver in a carjack situation.

with their backup lights on? What happens when the light changes and they hit the gas, forgetting they put the car in reverse? Try explaining that you didn't rear-end them, when no one comes forward as a witness.

Dash cams are a simple thing to add to your lineup of self-protection tools, and they come in enough varieties that even the most budget-conscious can afford one, while the techno-geeks have their share of feature-rich gadgets to choose from, as well. I think dash cams will probably become more common in the near future, and I encourage you to consider getting one to provide a little more security and defensive control to your drive.

9. Firearms and Carrying Them

So far I've talked primarily about the mindset I think any self-aware woman should have as she goes about her daily life, whether she chooses to go armed only with non-lethal defense tools or decides that carrying a firearm is the right choice for her. When you get down to it, none of those tools will work in your favor if you haven't trained yourself to use them, haven't been paying attention to what's going on around you and preparing to use them if a situation is about to escalate and, in the case of a firearm, haven't prepared yourself mentally for the possibility of taking another life in defense of your own or a loved one's life.

But let's assume that, if you've gotten this far in the book, you've chosen to carry. If you've never purchased a gun before or experienced only minimal exposure to firearms and shooting, you're going to be faced with hundreds of options. Entire volumes have been written on what guns are best for carry, and I'd tell you to browse through one or two such books—but since dozens of new models and variations are introduced each year, I'd tell you your next best bet is to get to a good retail shop and gun range.

Finding the Experts to Work With You

A great many of today's firearms retailers are as progressive as any other kind of retailer. The good ones are invested heavily in inventory and staff, and they are respected businesses involved in their communities. But, they are also like any other retailer in that there are ones who don't provide customer service or carry the goods you need (and don't really care).

While women are buying guns in ever-increasing numbers, some of the men behind the counter haven't picked up on that yet. Now, you wouldn't allow yourself to be told by a clerk in Home Depot that he won't sell you a lawnmower without having your husband with you, so don't put up with a firearms retailer who offers you only a micro .380 semi-automatic or a snub-nosed .38 Special revolver with a set of pink grips, because they're the only ones meant for "the little lady." In fact, if it's your first time buying a handgun and this happens to you, get out of that store as quickly as you can.

Really, you just need to do your homework the same way you would with other retailers. The first thing to do is find a store that has a large inventory of handguns and the staff to go with it. The staff needs to acknowledge you when you come through the door and walk up to the counter—but you need to take it from there. Be up front. Tell them what experience you have and don't have. The clerk, in turn, should ask you about your day-to-day life and what you want the gun for: Is it for self-defense, target shooting, both? Where do you go on your time off, what neighborhoods do you frequent during the work week? Do you work the midnight shift or nine-to-five, bad part of town or upscale office towers? He or she should also ask how you expect to carry your firearm. Should it be in a carry purse, inside-the-waistband holster, other type of holster?

With this kind of basic information exchanged, you should expect to be shown several guns that might work for you. Ask the clerk to explain their function if you're unfamiliar with the models being shown, as well as ammunition. Heck, ask him to do it even if you *do* know—if you're new to this, you're interviewing the store to see what kind of knowledge and service they can provide to you.

Have some options? Good. Go find another store and repeat the process. Try your local small retailer and try the big-box stores like Cabela's and Bass Pro. Try however many stores you need to until you find a retailer who understands the needs of a woman looking for a self-defense gun, including training, accessories, and where to find supportive and friendly ranges on which to practice.

A note about shooting ranges. Many ranges have rental guns available for use by their customers. By all means, and again, especially if you're new to handling handguns, take advantage of that. Even if they don't have the exact model you're considering buying, another model similar in shape, size, weight, and caliber can serve the purpose of getting you familiar with a gun's controls (can you reach them and activate them comfortably without altering your proper grip on the gun?), recoil during fire, and loading and unloading. You should try several. The more guns you shoot, the quicker you'll discover which models and calibers really appeal to you. From there you can narrow down the list to those that best accommodate how you want to carry.

The Myth of the "Little Lady" Gun

When it comes to concealed carry, the smaller the gun the better, right?

Not always. Maybe not even most of the time. Even in the smallest caliber generally available, the .22 LR, a small gun is going to be tough to shoot. Take that same small gun and chamber it for a caliber better suited to self-defense, and you can have a real handful of difficult-to-shoot gun.

It's a matter of basic physics. All other things being equal—caliber, your grip on the gun, etc.—a small and light gun will produce felt-recoil to a much higher degree than will a heavier, bigger gun. Tiny guns are hard on the hands, and can be very unpleasant to shoot.

Very small guns do have their place in your repertoire of self-defense tools. But you must understand that they are, as a whole, not a lot of fun to shoot, and that, in addition to being problematic when it comes to getting a proper grip on them in the first place, can also make them difficult to be accurate with. There's a bigger problem with them, too. When we have a gun that's not a lot of fun to shoot, we tend not to practice with it. And when you don't practice with a firearm that's already inherently difficult to be proficient with, then can you imagine how much tougher it might be to successfully defend yourself with one?

So does that leave you with full-size guns or even medium-sized guns? No, not necessarily. There are pluses and minuses to *every* gun choice for concealed carry. Too small and it's difficult and unpleasant to shoot. Too big and it'll feel heavy, bulky, and require a serious belt to secure it when you holster it, or it will always feel like a burden when you have it on you—and then you will stop carrying it, because it's just too much hassle, and then you won't have it when you need it.

Okay, the point to all this is that what I don't want you to do is get corralled into buying a small gun by some chauvinistic and uneducated salesperson who thinks you're delicate and can't handle a "real" gun. While today's firearms retailers as a whole are much more knowledgeable about their female customers and their capabilities, there's this pervasive myth among many that women shooters don't have the strength to manipulate the slide of a semi-auto and can't handle anything more than a five-shot .38 Special snub-nosed revolver. Both myths need to go away. Manipulating the slide of most common and popular self-defense semi-autos isn't any harder than picking up your purse and swinging it over your shoulder. In fact, some people with arthritis actually have an easier time with a semi-automatic—both in operating the slide and other controls, as well as in handling recoil— than they do loading and shooting those small-frame, short-barreled revolvers. As for those snubbies, well, they sure aren't what I'd call a pleasure to shoot in a .38 Special, especially the ultra-lightweight aluminum alloy- and titanium-framed models.

If you do choose a small gun as the one you want to keep with you regularly for self-defense, hit the range, hit it often, and get training with it. But also acquire a full-size gun you really *enjoy* shooting and shoot it *a lot*. Shoot it more than you do your carry gun, but each time you go to the range, finish each session with the fun gun by shooting a disciplined twenty-five or fifty practice shots with the not-so-fun gun.

There's a method to the madness. With a gun you really like, you'll end up going to the range more, and when you're having a good time, all of a sudden that short-barreled, little, hard-to-handle sidepiece isn't as daunting or challenging—or even as unpleasant—to shoot as it once was.

One more thing. Just because it's got a set of pink grips on it doesn't mean it's meant more for you than the model with the cushy black Hogue rubber grips (which are likely also more comfortable and functional). Pink (purple, green, leopard, and a rainbow of colors and patterns) abounds these days, when it comes to marketing firearms to women, but the majority of it, in my humble opinion, is nothing more than cosmetic marketing.

Holsters are a Must

The purpose of a holster is to secure your firearm safely while providing you access to it when you need it. It should fit your specific gun, cover the trigger, and provide enough retention so that your gun doesn't fall out during normal activity or in a physical scuffle.

There are a wide variety of holster carry methods, both on- and off-body. Let's discuss off-body carry first.

Off-body carry simply means your gun will be held in a holster that is not attached to your body or clothing. These can be purses, briefcases, or other totes enhanced with integral holster compartments. There are also backpacks and day planner-type cases that have holsters built into them, and I've even seen models that attach to the sideboards of your bed for quick access when you're facing an attack in your own home. (Note that such holsters are *never* to be an option when children or any other unauthorized and unknowing person is in your home.)

Though off-body holsters provide options, there are also some drawbacks. As you might imagine, they're more vulnerable to theft, as in a purse snatching, and you *must* be extra vigilant to keep it under your control *at all times*. Leaving your day planner/holster in the conference room would rank high on the irresponsibility list, and you can't leave a holster backpack hanging on a knob in the café where every other person hangs their backpack. With the purse holsters, you can't hang one on a chair in a restaurant, set it down where it can easily be grabbed by others, and you can't leave it in a shopping cart as you wander up and down the grocery store

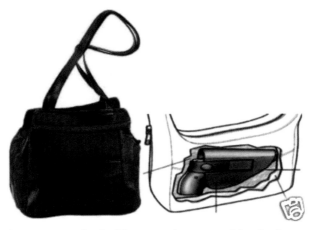

A carry purse looks like any other purse; it's what's inside that counts.

aisle. I'll say it again: It needs to be under your personal and full control and supervision *at all times.* This is for your safety and the safety of those around you.

Vehicle Carry

Another off-body carry option is vehicle carry. There are many options that provide holster carry while driving, including an arrangement that attaches under the steering wheel, and there are designs to fit the center console or attach handily to the side of the console or seat. Some people tuck this kind of holster between the seat and console, although I prefer a little more security. A sudden slamming of the brakes to avoid an accident can send such a holster flying, and that's definitely unsafe.

When considering a holster that attaches some-where in your vehicle, ease of access is key. Think about what would happen if you were trapped in your car and needed to defend yourself. Will you be restrained or become tangled in your seat belts? Can you access it without reaching over into the next seat (say, for a handgun holstered in the glove compartment), behind your seat, or even under your seat, which might be very difficult to do when strapped in by your seatbelt? How fast you can access your firearm in whichever method you choose to holster it in your vehicle is also a consideration. Some of the center-console holsters also double as in-car safes (with either a key or cypher lock), and while these can be smart things if you can't take your firearm into a particular building and must leave it in your vehicle, you do have to consider how quickly you can access the gun once you're behind the wheel and driving.

There are two final things to consider about made-for-vehicle holsters. The first is that they are designed only to hold your firearm securely and safely in one place that you can access it quickly. They are not meant to store the gun there when you are not in your vehicle, as most provide at least a partial view of the firearm to those adept at quickly studying vehi-cle interiors. The second consideration, as I discussed earlier, is that of discretion. Do not make a big deal of taking your gun out of your on-body holster or purse holster and securing it in your vehicle holster. The less attention you attract when performing such tasks the better. If you are not concerned about concealing your gun in the car, there is a new product that looks like a travel mug, fits into the cup holder, and holds your gun muzzle down. Effective, but not very discreet.

There are so many options with on-body carry, they can make your head spin. There are, literally, hundreds and hundreds of holsters out there, made from a number of materials and meant to be carried or secured to your body in just about any place you can imagine. As a way to help you work your way through the myriad options, let's talk about the major on-body holster categories:

- Shoulder—Looks cool in the movies but can be challenging to control (they're not very stable, not being firmly attached to a piece of clothing), draw from, and conceal. Many people who wear a jacket or blazer all day and are confined for long hours in a vehicle or office chair can find this design to be highly comfortable.
- Ankle—These come in several forms, from a lacy sleeve or a leather rig with a garter to a holster that attaches around your ankle with Velcro. They can be a very good option for a smaller or backup gun, and they do work well if you have good flexibility and are able to get up and down quickly. If you have trouble bending at the waist or touching your toes, either from a standing or sitting position, an ankle holster may not be the best option for you. I have artificial knees, which makes it challenging to kneel or rise quickly. That

makes an ankle holster a poor option for me. If you can't get to it without help, it won't be good for you. Keep in mind, too, that ankle holsters also require a lot of getting used to, as your pants need to be long enough to cover one, even when seated. You also may have to learn to walk a little differently, making sure not to bang your ankles together when you walk.

- Small-of-the-Back (SOB)—This holster works for many people, but you do need enough flexibility in your arms and shoulders to reach around behind you. It's a good recommendation from a concealed perspective, especially if you wear a blazer or other loose over-garment regularly. However, it's not likely the most comfortable holster to wear if you are sitting behind the wheel of a vehicle or in an office chair all day. It is not my recommended method, however, because if you are knocked down and fall backward, your gun is between the ground and your spine. Assuming you are not injured by the fall, you are still laying on your gun, and if your attacker is quickly on you, you'll not have much chance of retrieving it. A better option? Look for a similarly designed holster that positions itself over the kidney. This way the gun is still behind you, but mid-way between your spine and hip.

- Outside-the-Waistband (OWB)—This is a holster that clips over your belt or a sturdy waistband—and I do mean sturdy, because anything otherwise and, with the exception of all but the lightest guns and holsters, the weight of the gun will lean it away from your body, which will neither help conceal it nor have the gun in the best position from which to draw. As you might imagine from its name, this holster style holds your gun outside your pants. They can be worn in a variety of positions, most commonly at the hip. It is a more common holster selection for people who open carry (i.e., do not try to conceal their gun), though, with a little care (again, a regularly worn blazer, jacket, or other topping garment), you can effectively conceal this type of holster and your gun. My top pick and one I use frequently is a Safariland (www.safariland.com) paddle holster with thumb break.

- Inside-the-Waistband (IWB)—This is a holster that fits between you and the waistband of your pants or skirt. It attaches either via a clip or with loops that come over the top of your waistband and fasten around a belt, those loops secured with snaps. I like this holster style for appendix carry. Picture a clock face with your navel as 12:00. Appendix carry is generally at the 10:00 to 11:00 or 1:00 to 2:00 o'clock position (depending on whether you are right- or left-handed and if you are strong-side drawing or cross-drawing). Hip carry positions range from 2:00 to 4:00 or 8:00 to 11:00 o'clock, as people will carry slightly forward of the hip, on the hip, or slightly behind the hip. My favorite IWB is the AVA from Flashbang Holsters (www. flashbangholster.com).

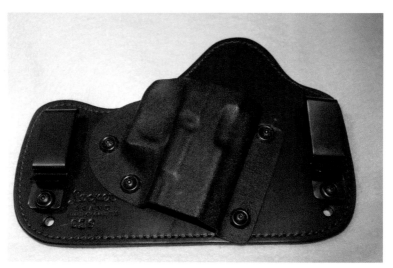

AVA holster.

- Belly Band or Compression Band—This holster is a stretchy band that wraps around your mid-section or pelvis, usually secures with Velcro or a hook-and-eye closure, and contains pockets to carry the gun and at least one spare magazine. They come in a variety of sizes and styles, and they work well under clothing that lacks a strong waistband, such as workout gear. I prefer the models that have silicone strips on the inside, which help keep them from sliding once adjusted into place. I often use a Sport Belt from Can Can Concealment (www.cancanconcealment.com).

- Bra Holsters—There are several manufactures making bra holsters now. They tend to work best with very compact guns, as the holster component generally attaches to the center of the bra, with the gun tucked up under the bottom band. At least one maker contains its holster within the bra cup itself. For the center arrangement, you draw by reaching under your shirt and pulling down on the gun's grip. For the cup model, roughly the same thing, though if you have a scoop-necked shirt or other top that's open at the neck and

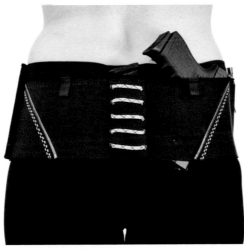

Compression band holster. Photo Courtesy of Can Can Concealment.

cleavage, you can more easily reach in through that opening and locate the gun quite easily within the bra cup. Some women love these, some don't.

- Pocket—These are, essentially, sleeves, generally sized to a gun type, that can be tucked into a pocket, be carried in a tight waistband without a clip (be careful in the restroom; as soon as you release the tension, it will fall), or in a coat pocket. These holsters mostly accommodate those very small micro and mouse guns intended for concealed carry. A Remora (www.remoraholsterstore.com) pocket holster is one of my favorites to carry with a small gun.

There are other holster types and designs, and the many manufacturers are always coming up with new designs. Holsters also come in myriad materials, from plain cowhide and exotic leathers to Kydex or ballistic nylon, and some holsters have a combination of materials. They all have their advantages and disadvantages. Nylon, for instance, is very lightweight, but holsters made from these materials tend to have a finite lifespan. Eventually, the foam interiors become compressed,

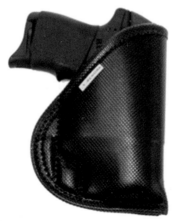

Pocket Holsters, available in a variety of sizes and materials, can be very handy.

the holster loses its internal shape, and then the gun is sloppy on the inside, which can lead to it falling out too easily or provide an easy grab by a bad guy in a physical altercation. Leather can last for decades, generally keeping its shape with care, and without the same degree of loosening that nylon holsters experience. However, leather is heavy, can be hot and more uncomfortable in general when worn against the body, as it's more rigid, and leather holsters are generally much more expensive than nylon.

How do you know what holster is right for you? Trial and error is the only way to know, but as you sort through the varieties keep in mind that one holster rarely does all jobs. Let's say, for instance, that you've chosen an ankle rig as your primary daily carry holster option. What do you do on those days you want to wear a skirt, or shorts on the weekend? Consider, too, that unless you live in those regions of California or Florida where the weather doesn't fluctuate much, you're going to have wide variety of clothing on across the four seasons. If you carry concealed, "printing"—the ability of others to detect the outline of your gun through your clothing—is a real concern when your garments are tight and lightweight (summer clothing), and sometimes when your garment is flowing and a breeze or wind presses the fabric against the gun and holster. (With any holster and concealed carry, you must also be aware of your regular movements potentially pulling a covering garment away from your body or the wind blowing the garment to the side and revealing the butt of the gun to onlookers.)

So, if one holster won't do the job all the time, then what? For almost anyone who carries on a regular basis, it's easier to just give in and realize that holsters are like black high heels: You can own twenty pairs and still not have the right pair in your closet for that one occasion. And that's okay! Your clothing changes, how you come and go changes, your vehicles change, and your weight changes. Your gun will often change, too. With all those changes will come changes in your holster.

In addition to understanding that change is inevitable, you also need to keep in mind that every time you change one of these elements—clothes, gun, holster, and carry position— you will need to train to be safe and efficient with that new combination. This is especially important if you have been carrying your gun one way for a long time. When you practice regularly, muscle memory comes into play, and that's a good thing, because it eventually makes the process of sweeping away your jacket edge, getting your hand on the butt of your gun, and getting the gun drawn and into position a very efficient (read, "fast") process. But let's say you've changed from that right-hip carry to a shoulder rig because you've just switched jobs and are now in your car off and on all day traveling to job sites. Sure, you *know* your gun is in a new location, but have you practiced drawing from it? That gun in a shoulder rig is oriented in a manner completely different from hip carry. Have you practiced pulling a magazine from its position on that shoulder rig? You need to, because that spare mag isn't where it was before.

Practice, as it is with all things firearms and other defensive tools, is the path to success. Lots of time on the range, lots of time dry-firing and working your ways through various scenarios, will be critical to your ability to survive an encounter. Practice builds skills and it builds the speed with which you can deploy those skills, and with that comes confidence. No, no one truly knows what they're going to do when the chaos of a violent attack erupts. Not even law enforcement. When bad things happen, the situation rarely unfolds along predictable lines, so street officers do get caught off-guard and they do get injured. It's not for a lack of training, but rather a lack of a crystal ball. You have to be realistic and understand that it's simply not possible to train, nor expect, every type of bad thing that can happen to us. Just as you can't stay in a state of hyper-alertness all the time. However, it is absolutely possible to train for *some* of what life might hand you, and that can go a long way towards saving your life one day.

Why Holster-Less is Never an Option

Earlier in this chapter I stated that a holster was necessary to securing your firearm safely, while also providing you access to it when you need it. I also said that it should fit your specific gun, cover the trigger, and provide retention so that your gun doesn't fall out during normal activity or in a scuffle.

The inclination with many, especially with the carry of super-compact semi-autos and small, five-shot revolvers, is to simply dump the gun in your purse or slip it in the front pocket of a loose-fitting pair of trousers or coat. Don't do this—ever.

In a purse, your firearm can become lost in the jumble of other things you carry. Not only could you have trouble locating the gun at all, you could grab it by the wrong end. You also run the risk of other items getting caught in the trigger guard, which could then accidentally and negligently discharge the firearm. You will encounter the same problem with a very small gun in a large pocket—think about how easy it is for your keys to get tangled in an un-holstered gun. Also, without a holster, firearms stashed in pockets or purses rarely stay oriented in the position you need them to be in, and then it becomes too easy to slip your finger though that trigger guard as you withdraw the weapon.

Retention—the grip of the holster around the gun—is the other benefit of a holster. It refers mostly to those holsters worn on the body. Holsters come in a variety of retention levels. Those that law enforcement utilize have components built into them that prevent the gun from falling out of the holster during a physical altercation and which make a gun grab by an opponent almost impossible. Drawing quickly and efficiently from such holsters requires *significant* training, because there's very little leeway with draw angle and technique if one wants the gun to come out of the holster at all.

So what level of retention do you need? One that enables you to quickly draw and position the gun to fire without the gun accidentally falling out of it during your normal activities or those circumstances you think you might find yourself in. Again, this could mean more than one holster for you. Best recommendation? Find that retail store that's well-stocked with holsters of all shapes and carry positions and talk to a knowledgeable staff member about their picks. Though any holster is more comfortable once it's broken in (and that includes broken in to fit the gun—leather holsters can be very tight initially and often require some working of the gun in and out of them before the gun doesn't "stick"), ask to try on the ones that interest you, working with a dummy gun or your own gun unloaded. Can you easily reach behind you and grasp your gun from a behind-the back model? How far do you have to lift the gun from a hip-side IWB holster before it clears your clothing and the holster itself, and does the gun uncomfortably catch the side of your breast when you draw? If the answers to those questions are your armpit and "yes," you likely need to try an appendix carry or shoulder rig. The good news is that there *are* so many options. You are not stuck with just a half-dozen models designed for guys 6-foot 4-inches that you'll have to "make work" for you. Try one, try three, and keep trying them until you find the ones that work the best for you. I promise, it'll be almost as much fun as searching for that perfect pair of black high heels.

10. Carrying While Physically Challenged

It will happen to almost everyone at some point in their life. You will become injured or weakened by illness. Your vision will do the opposite of improve, just as will your hearing and even your sense of smell. Even if you make it to a ripe old age without a trip to the ER or a case of the common cold, that aging itself has its effects (and in my case, it's not happening so gracefully). You will get slower, you will lose strength, you will not have the elasticity in your joints and muscles you had in your youth.

Ailments may be permanent or temporary, minor or severe; it's not uncommon anymore to see veterans regaining their lives after traumatic injuries, such as the loss of a limb. But what about you? Maybe you're on crutches, using a cane, recovering from a stroke, weakened by cancer, balancing a baby on your hip (yes, this can be an impairment), pregnant, dealing with a catastrophic injury or maybe something as annoying as a broken wrist. Despite any and all of these things and the hundreds, thousands of things that keep us from going about our lives at 100 percent physical perfection, the one thing we all have in common is the desire to defend ourselves and be safe. So how do you do that when not all of your body's cooperating? Let's look at a few examples of physical impairments and how some people found the workaround that allowed them to continue to carry a firearm.

When You're Physically Injured

Being the consummate klutz, I have found myself incapacitated more than once. I've been on crutches, I've stepped down (no pun intended) to a cane multiple times, and I've had, at different times, either hand in a cast, as well as shoulder injuries that left me in a sling for weeks at a time. I do understand the feeling of vulnerability that comes with being impaired, and the need to adapt.

One of the most common examples of an impairment or limitation that I've seen as an instructor is a hand limitation. I worked with someone quite recently who was recovering from a stroke and had lost most of the control in his dominant hand. He still wanted to keep his trusty .38 for home defense, but asked for advice on how to hold it. I encouraged him to practice with his left hand, which was unaffected by the stroke, and that proved to be a sound solution for him.

I've put too much wear and tear on my hips and have small tears in the lining, among other issues. For a while, that meant I had to use a cane. Do you know what looks more vulnerable than a fifty-plus-year-old woman limping through a parking lot? A fifty-plus-year-old woman limping through a parking lot with a cane. I had to adjust how I carried while using that cane, and I also had to work to figure out how to keep my balance while I used the cane to create distance from an attacker and give me a chance to do something else (because running wasn't really an option at that point).

What do these two stories have in common? Limitations and identifying workarounds. The workaround to your limitation may be more complex than either mine or my friend's, but you can almost always find one. Short of being so incapacitated you need a full-time caregiver, it may take a little out-of-the-box thinking, but you can nearly always find the tools and ways to use them to defend yourself.

A major consideration when you are injured is where to carry your gun. For instance, you may need to adapt your carry location based on your aids. On crutches? Pretty much rules out hip carry (more on that in a bit). Is your arm in a sling? Probably need to carry on the other side or possibly in the sling itself. You'll also need to accommodate extra magazines or moon clips and speedloaders and learn how to safely reload your gun with just one hand if the other is out of commission.

Something else you'll need to consider is that recovering from an illness won't generally necessitate a change in your carry method, but it will likely mean you'll need to work on your stamina and control as you recover. Just be patient, realizing you'll need build your stamina and strength over time. You didn't lose it in a day, and you won't regain it overnight.

Carrying While Pregnant or With Children

Many parents with small children want to carry concealed firearms, but struggle with where on their bodies to carry the firearm, because their arms are so often full of the children themselves. The most common solution I've found, after interviewing many parents, is the appendix carry. This carry position gives you quick access to your gun, if you're carrying the child or infant in the arm that's not attached to your strong hand (which is typical of most adults carrying a child). It is also the easiest carry style if you are constantly bending up and down to deal with the kiddos, and it gives you the most control when you are bending down or forward, as you won't be exposing your gun, something that would happen if you were carrying your firearm in a holster positioned behind your back. Finally, appendix carry more readily encourages you to keep your free hand near or on the gun itself and, therefore, small hands away. When carrying with children, consider some additional retention in your holster, such as the SafariLand ALS. You want a mechanism that is easily accessed to release the firearm, but not easily accessed by small children. Unless you practice often, and even though there are accidents, I would shy away from a holster that requires you to use your trigger finger to disengage the retention. The Serpa is a fine holster but many shooters have accidently shot themselves in the leg trying to draw their gun.

Pregnancy is an impairment, defensively speaking. Your center of gravity shifts as you gain pregnancy weight, and you may feel awkward and off balance late in the term. If you find this to be the case, practice drawing and dry-firing while seated, as well as doing the same while rising to stand, which many pregnant women find difficult to do during the last few months.

Women who are pregnant and wish to carry do need to be aware of chemical and lead exposure when handling ammunition and firearms (particularly their cleaning solvents and lubricants). It's a good idea to have someone else clean your guns if you're shooting regularly while pregnant, or at least wear rubber gloves. Depending on you and your doctor, you may actually want to avoid live shooting and the inescapable exposure to lead. That doesn't mean you can't train, but utilize a training dummy gun or dry-fire practice.

As your shape changes during pregnancy, carrying with many holsters can become challenging, or even impossible. Enter the compression band or belly band holster as a great option. It can be shifted to wrap under an expanding abdomen and positioned to allow carry on the hip or in the kidney area. Indeed, it is likely the easiest carry method once you have a prominent baby bump.

Aging (Gracefully or Otherwise)

It is said that aging isn't an impairment, but rather a reward for surviving. Still, as we age, many things can change. Strength and stability lessen, tremors can appear, and visual, auditory, and olfactory clarity dissipate. All of these naturally occurring signs of age can impact

Use a Gripmaster to strengthen hands and fingers.

your shooting—and yet nearly all, at least on some level, can be worked through.

Hand-strengthening devices, such as the one made by Gripmaster (www.prohands.net), can work wonders at building finger and hand strength that can improve trigger control, enhance the handling recoil, and aid in manipulating safeties, slides, decocker levers, hammers, cylinder releases, and other gun parts.

Building your torso's core muscles will increase your overall stability, which provides the platform that enables you to fire a gun accurately and which is required in the use of semi-autos so that their actions fully cycle. That doesn't mean you have to turn to Crossfit in your seventies, but find a personal trainer experienced with working with the skeletons and musculature of those past the mid-age point and hit the gym.

Tremors, that uncontrollable shaking that so often accompanies our later years, can be very frustrating for a shooter. Yet I've worked with students who had significant hand tremors and were great shooters. They had learned to work *with* the tremor, instead of fighting against it. For instance, they figured out that the longer the gun is held at full extension, the more likely a tremor will increase as fatigue sets in; they therefore factor in frequent breaks when they're practicing.

Finally, eyeglasses and hearing aids can compensate for much of the sensory loss that accompanies our later years, though I've also worked with students who were completely deaf, and it had no impact on their ability to shoot. There is a point where your vision may fail you enough to prevent handling firearms, but that doesn't mean those intermediate devices I talked about earlier in this book aren't still options.

Sensory Underload—And When to Say When

We depend on our collective senses to keep us out of trouble. When one of those senses begins to slip, the others will have to pick up the slack. This is especially true when it comes to RPA and situational awareness.

Your auditory faculties are perhaps the easiest for which to compensate. Yes, hearing aids can be a wonderful fix, but they are also expensive and rarely covered by insurance plans. Too, they aren't perfect devices. The father of a friend of mine has a pair of high-tech and very pricey hearing aids. They work wonderfully—when they're working. But they emit a high-pitched squeal when the batteries are dying, and, according to the friend, those batteries tend to have a short shelf life. Her father compensates for that added frustration by simply not even putting in his hearing aids many days, and he generally takes them out at night to save the batteries.

Now, my friend's father doesn't keep a gun for home protection, but, if he did, can you see where his hearing loss and hearing aid habits have him at a disadvantage? How would he hear someone breaking into the house at night? How would he hear someone coming up behind him?

If this were my father, who kept a firearm for self-defense and otherwise had no trouble safely and accurately handling that gun (and even if he didn't keep a gun), I'd sit down and have a talk with him about wearing his hearing aids at night, for starters. But then I'd also suggest he change his habits when he was out and about, perhaps altering travel routes to pass through safer neighborhoods, and I'd certainly encourage him to spend more time *looking* around him wherever he went.

Vision loss presents a different set of challenge than auditory loss does. Eyeglasses can correct only so much. Too, you have to consider what you are capable of doing with a handgun if your glasses are not available. What if you're attacked and your glasses are knocked off your face? You may still be capable of handling your firearm, but can you see what you're aiming at? What about innocent bystanders? How about in the middle of the night? Is that an intruder—or is it your grandchild quietly coming in your room to tell you she needs a glass of water? Remember, putting on your glasses to see requires your hands, dexterity, and time. If it's an intruder, that time might be too long. And if you don't put them on and it's your grandchild or the family dog . . .

At some point, loss of vision will mandate that a firearm can no longer be your self-defense tool. So, too, will the loss of tactile sensation in the hands and maybe even the arms. If you can't feel the gun, you can neither safely retrieve it from a holster or safe, nor safely fire it. In either case, continuing to keep a firearm for self-protection greatly increases the risk of that firearm being used against you. Should the loss of either your vision or your ability to physically feel, grip, aim, and pull the trigger happen to you and you are otherwise mentally sound, it would be wise to consider divesting yourself of your firearms and seeking other means of self-defense.

Using Your Mobility Aids

I talked earlier about my periodic need for a cane and how that impacted how I carried my firearm. But even if I hadn't had the ability to carry a firearm, the cane itself could have come to my rescue.

It is important to understand that mobility aids can be useful to you in a defensive capacity. Like anything else, such tactics take practice, but, in this case, I would encourage you to use extreme caution, including having someone to help steady you until you feel comfortable with the maneuvers. It is, it should go without saying, important to try them *before*

Straight, collapsible, curved, crooked . . . canes can keep you mobile.

you need them, so you can figure out what works best for you and your injury, which will increase your likelihood of coming out of an attack on the winning time. In fact, if you haven't practiced, you might be better off not resisting an attack unless you believe yourself to be in serious danger. Once you resist, the fight is on, and you can't reset back to a less violent posture.

One note: The first time you try a defensive move with whatever mobility aid you have should not be done at full speed against an able-bodied aggressor. That makes *you* more likely to be injured, and likely worse than you are already.

Many of the ideas and injuries described below are and were mine. Okay, I'm someone who can trip over a shadow, but, the point is that, when your normal carry method doesn't work, you need to be ready to change your plan. To a criminal, someone with an obvious injury looks like a weaker target. Be prepared to defend yourself in new ways.

Crutches

In a previous chapter, I mentioned my broken toe. Many of us break toes regularly enough that it isn't a big deal, but, in that particular instance, I broke all three bones, the last one being crushed. That meant I had to stay off of it for a while to let it heal (which it did, and I avoided surgery), but enter the dreaded crutches.

The only good thing I can say about crutches is that they give you amazing, crack-a-walnut biceps. However, for strong-sided carry on the hip, crutches are the worst. (Really, you

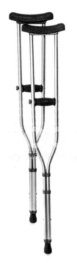

Crutches present carry problems, but there are ways to do it.

can't get to either hip easily.) I played with the idea of a bra holster, but settled on carrying appendix.

If you have never carried in the appendix position (in front of the hip bone), it takes some getting used to. On crutches, it tends to work particularly well if you position the holster on the side opposite your injury. This gives you the easiest access to your gun in a critical situation. If this isn't your normal carry position, you do need to practice, as the draw stroke is different and the crutch will still be slightly in the way. I found the sweet spot for me, where the gun was just forward enough not to catch a crutch while I was either drawing the gun or while in motion on the crutches, but still easily accessed if I dropped a crutch and balanced on the other. Then it was time to practice.

When practicing, remember that you may need to drop your crutch to get to your gun—and that means you need to be prepared to be knocked backward and possibly fall when you drop that crutch. Still, the second gained may be all you need to get to your gun. If you can stay on your feet and draw, great, but so long as you can maintain control of your firearm as you fall and hit the ground, you can still be in position to fire. I prefer to practice with a blue gun, but an unloaded and triple-checked firearm can be used for dry-fire practice as well. I practiced walking, sitting, and standing while drawing and aiming without causing myself to fall over. I started out by being close to a wall, so that I could catch myself and stay upright if I lost my balance and until I got used to accommodating my draw while balancing on the crutch.

Handling a gun while on crutches wasn't the only thing I practiced. I also learned how to defensively use the crutch itself. Can you keep your balance while thrusting or swinging a crutch at an assailant, in order to buy time to get to your gun? For those of you who have never had the pleasure of being on crutches, it sounds easy, but it sure isn't! When you start to practice swinging a crutch, have someone near you (behind, preferably) to catch you so you don't fall while you practice and develop some skills.

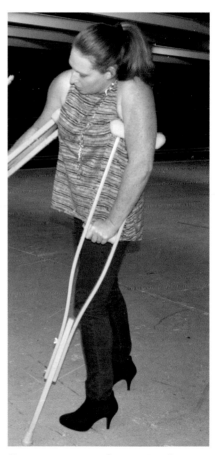

To get a defensive stance on crutches, you will bring the crutch of your injured side slightly forward and to the center of your body, just a few inches, and then cant or angle it inward (toward your center), about 20 to 30 degrees. Lean heavily on this crutch for support. Doing this helps give you a more stable platform from which to

Lean on one crutch to maintain a defensive posture.

respond with a firearm, and it provides you the best stability in the event you want to use your strong-side crutch as a defensive tool. It also leaves the uninjured leg free to help you regain your balance, if needed.

You can use your crutch to put some distance between you and an attacker. Use it as an extension of your arm and thrust hard into the center chest (solar plexus) of your aggressor to punch them backwards. This moves needs to be quick, decisive, and *hard*. You may also be able to sweep their knees with a crutch, thus knocking down your attacker.

Once again, your safety and that of innocent bystanders around you is the key concern. If you do not feel steady enough to practice these techniques, don't! If you do, ensure

You can use a crutch to sweep the knee of an attacker.

you have someone to help steady you as you work through the moves in slow motion and gain a level of comfort before you increase your speed and force.

Canes

Canes can be used in much the same way as crutches. However, when carrying a cane as an aid to walking, that cane is always used on the side *opposite* the injury, so you need to be cognizant of your stability.

You have more carry options for your firearm when you're using a cane, such as appendix, hip, kidney, shoulder carry, and small of back, but your gun should be on the side opposite your cane so you can reach it without having to drop the cane. If your cane hand is not your normal writing hand or strong side, you may need a new holster to orient your gun

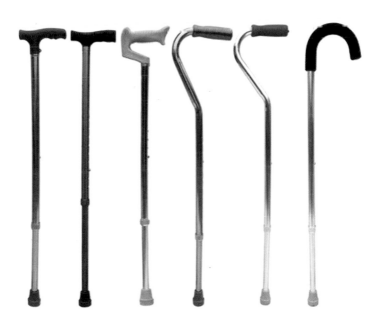

effectively, and you will need to practice carrying and drawing from your weak hand.

As its own defensive tool, a cane can be held by its handle and thrust to gain distance. If you do and the aggressor grabs your cane to wrestle it from you, you can shove forward—hard—and then yank back fast. This push-pull tactic can be very effective.

A second use for your cane is as a club. Practice tossing it straight up to catch the tip end, kind of like a magician's wand flourish, so that you can swing it like a bat, making sure to use the most solid end to hit the side of the head or the neck of your assailant. Consider which part of your cane is the most solid in this maneuver and use it accordingly. If you have a crook cane with a curved handle, it will be the straight

Use a cane to keep an attacker at a distance. Be prepared to shove it forward, then pull it back, should he try to grab it.

side. It you have a Derby handle, it is the shorter end with the handle.

Finally, another defensive use for the cane will be to hold it by its tip and then slip the handle end quickly between your assailant's legs and jerk forward, hooking him behind the knee. This should take him off balance and likely down to the ground.

Walkers

Walkers present their own challenges. I used one after having surgery on both knees at the same time (I could barely stand on my own). If your use of one is more for balance than mobility, you can effectively carry your firearm in almost any position, using one hand to steady yourself with the walker as you draw and fire. If, however, you need to lean heavily on your walker, as I did, you may want to minimize your exposure until you are more comfortable or recovered.

Arm Casts and Slings

Few things are as miserable as having a broken wing. Having one quickly makes it apparent how much we take our hands for granted, and it doesn't matter if it is a broken finger, carpal tunnel, wrist fracture, or a break at the elbow, shoulder, or collarbone—that arm is out of commission.

I once fell forward, throwing my hands out to break the fall, and fractured my right wrist. I ended up with a cast almost to the elbow that held my thumb out at an angle (a thumb spica cast). Such casting rendered my thumb useless to me and made shooting and even most two-handed gun

If one hand is in a cast, learn how to shoot one-handed . . .and practice!

manipulation impossible. The doctor put me in a sling. What's a gal to do?

Remember the discussion earlier in this chapter about becoming proficient with one-handed, weak-handed shooting? No choice *but* that for me. I managed it, though I struggled with reloads, which had become very difficult, as the cast prevented me from pinching my thumb and fingers together. Still, with patience and practice I managed, and just as I did, you can find a method that works for you.

Upper body appendage slings are necessary and useful to a variety of injuries. There are different types of slings, ranging from merely supportive types that hold the arm close to the body, to more complex designs that keep the injured limb at a specific angle, or those that brace and support the shoulder, for example. As it is with lower body injuries, your weak side is now your injured side, regardless whether that side is also your strong side.

One thing I learned when wearing a sling is they are a great place to stash small objects. It may be possible to conceal a compact pistol in one, provided it's protected by a holster, such as the Remora pocket holster. Such a holster helps keep the firearm in place and oriented so that you can draw it effectively. Too, if the holster comes out with the gun when you draw, you can quickly knock it off. Keep in mind that, if you choose to conceal a small gun in your sling, you do need to both practice and be vigilant about sweeping others around you with the muzzle of the gun, as you are, essentially, drawing "cross-body." Such a draw also puts your brachial artery in the line of fire, so the firearms safety tenet of keeping your finger off the trigger until ready to shoot is paramount.

Depending on your injury, and as it is with things like crutches and canes, you may be able to use the injured arm as a block, especially if that arm is in a cast. Yes, it's going to hurt, so be prepared, but it could connect well enough with an attacker to knock them off their balance or even unconscious. Do keep in mind that, if you have a shoulder injury, you are less likely to be able to use your arm to swing its cast at someone.

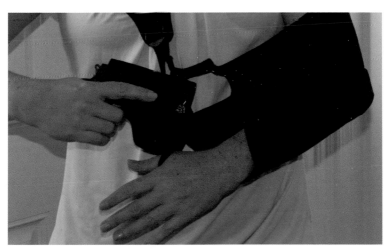

Slings are great places to stash things, including small pistols.

Other Considerations When All the Parts Aren't Working

As always, your awareness is your best defense. Minimize your exposure and your risk. If you know an area is dangerous, why go there when your own mobility is limited. Practice shooting one-handed and one-handed weak side (much more on this in the next chapter). It may be crucial to your survival.

At the same time, remember that your weak side isn't necessarily just the hand and arm opposite your normal writing hand. When injured or impaired, your weak side will be the side of your body that is suffering. For example, when I shattered my ankle and ended up in a cast, it was my right ankle. But I'm right-handed, so suddenly my right side was my weak side, defensively speaking. When I fractured a toe, badly, and was in a surgical boot, it was my left foot that was injured, so that became my weak side, defensively speaking.

One last thing to consider: if you find yourself on the ground, an aggressor may target the weaker side to cause you additional injury and pain in the hopes of making you more compliant. You want to protect your injured side as best you can, possibly rolling slightly to that side in an effort to minimize exposure to the injury while also giving you the best use of your strong side.

11. One-Handed Firearm Skills

If you have found yourself in any one of the situations presented in the last chapter, it doesn't take long to realize that a lot of injuries can leave you with only one useful hand. This is true even of lower body injuries, where a cane, crutches, or walker are required. If you're limited to use of only one hand, then you need to be proficient shooting with that hand.

One-handed shooting is most certainly a skill-level up from two-handed, and if that one hand is your non-writing, weak hand, the required skill level goes up again. Let's look at some tips to help acquire those skills so that you can connect with an intended target.

If one hand is occupied, either with your mobility aid or because of injury, you need to be prepared to reload or clear a malfunction. This isn't easy, and may best be learned watching a video, and there are some great ones on YouTube. I recommend searching for "One-Handed Reload" by Mike Seeklander. Mike has an extensive background as a professional trainer and is great at breaking the steps down in an easy to follow way.

Working with Full Arm Extension

If you are able to extend whatever single arm you have to full extension, you'll want to cant the gun slightly toward the center of your body. No, you don't want to hold it sideways a la "gangsta" mode, but you should tilt it inwards off its perpendicular center line so that the gun's top line is between 1:00 and 2:00 o'clock for right-handed shooting (10:00 and 11:00 o'clock for left-handed). This bit of canting will give your wrist more stability, allowing you to recover from recoil faster while still allowing you to use your sights as you would if the gun were vertical (i.e., you can still line up the front sight in the notch of the rear and focus on the front sight).

Working from the Bent Arm Position

Shooting one-handed with the shooting arm bent means that you could very well be shooting from the hip. The good news is that it's easier than it sounds (though you may need permission from your range facility to practice this technique).

To effectively shoot from the hip, keep your arm close to your body (this helps maximize your stability and provides some steadiness to the gun), and understand fully that where your hand is pointed is where you are aiming—you won't be using the gun's sights, so it is critical that you are completely aware of exactly where your muzzle is oriented.

In addition to being the only shooting method available to you due to an injury, shooting from the hip one-handed is a good skill to have in the event of a very close encounter. However, if you are shooting more than a few feet away and can extend your arm to utilize the sights, it is better to

This is an example of a close-quarter drill. If you practice something like this, you need to be extremely careful and keep your finger off the trigger, as the weak hand is ahead of the muzzle. Muzzle orientation is paramount and this should only be attempted with live fire by an experienced shooter.

push the gun out to full extension, which is a more stable and inherently accurate position.

If your range does not allow you to practice shooting from the hip, you may want to invest in a blue gun or a SIRT. I prefer the SIRT—shot indicating resetting trigger—dummy firearms because I can see where my "shots" are placed, helping me to verify my point of aim.

Reloading with One Hand

The techniques for clearing a malfunction or reloading with one hand are similar. Let's deal with the reload first, semi-automatics and then revolvers. Keep in mind that for either, you will have to find the places on you or near you where you can get to magazine and speedloaders not just easily, but in a manner that facilitates one-handed reloading.

Semi-Automatics—You will, of course, need to first get rid of the empty magazine in your gun. Drop the magazine— just let it fall. Don't worry about where it goes, don't worry about picking it up, just forget about it. If you're worried about damaging your magazines during practice, many magazines permit the use of bumper pads that can be affixed to their bottoms and that help protect them. They're in common use by those who shoot action sports like IPSC or 3-Gun, so seek out a gun shop that caters to these shooters or research these accessories online.

When you are in an emergency situation, hit that magazine release whichever way you can and let the magazine drop away. Forget about it, and leave it where it falls. It's empty and of no service to you, so focus on the reload and getting ready to shoot again.

How you eject your magazine may become important depending on how the controls of your gun are configured. Most handguns will have the magazine release on the left side of the gun for easy access by the thumb of a right-handed shooter. More guns are produced today with ambidextrous

Pistol with spare magazine.

magazine releases, and still other models allow for this control to be reversed, so, if you're shooting with your left hand, you'll want that release button relocated to the right side if possible.

What if you can't reverse the mag release and you have to shoot with your left hand? Then your reload is going to take patience and concentration. You may be able to adjust your grip so that you can depress the mag release button with your middle or index finger. If so, practice, practice, practice this. If you can't access the button this way, you'll need to insert the gun, possibly backward, into your holster, or between your knees, then press the button, and either pull out the magazine or pick up the gun and shake it loose. Alternately, if you are absolutely sure the gun is completely empty (the slide is locked back and you can visually see that no round is in the chamber or topping the magazine within), then you lay it down, and then depress the magazine release and remove the magazine.

Whether you set the gun down or brace it somewhere as I've just suggested, remember, you have only the one hand to both retrieve your

Here, a shooter practices one-handed reloading. He's tucked the semi-auto in between his knees after ejecting the empty mag, and oriented it so that he can easily insert the replacement magazine.

spare magazine and put it in the gun with that hand, then pick up the gun again to shoot. Always, *always* be careful of your muzzle orientation when maneuvering a gun from the unusual positions you may be forced to utilize in such a case—it can be incredibly easy to sweep parts of your own body and others around you.

You will also need to be cautious of slamming the magazine home to seat it properly, as some guns with touchy slide releases might have the slides cycle forward when a magazine is seated with force, and some may even slam-fire (although this is very rare in modern firearms)—and that can be a *catastrophic* event if you have the gun wedged somewhere on your body. To avoid the possibility of this happening, either set the gun down on a solid surface for the entire reload operation, or, if you've wedged the gun between your knees or between your arm cast and body, set the magazine almost fully, then grip the gun, point the barrel in a safe direction, and finish seating the mag by rapping the bottom of the magazine hard on your knee, table, cast, whatever's available. If your mags tend to be loosey-goosey and fall out of your pistol with ease when they're not fully set, you can keep your last finger and/ or pinky under the mag as you grip the gun and until you have the gun safely oriented. Then, hold the gun just high enough above the flat surface on which you intend to seat the mag to prevent it from falling out completely (and keeping you from having to start all over again), and bring the butt of your grip down on that surface.

Once you have a fresh magazine loaded in your pistol, you're going to need to get a round in the chamber. If the slide locked open because you ran the gun dry, then most people will instinctively hit the slide stop, adjust their grip, and prepare to shoot. If you did a tactical reload (meaning you had time to reload—either because you were able to get to cover or for some other reason that allowed you time—before you emptied your gun),

Placing a semi-auto backwards and upside down between the knees for reloading assists with re-gripping the gun.

then the gun's slide should be forward and there should be a live round in the chamber. A third scenario is that you ran the gun dry, but the slide either failed to lock back or you accidentally sent the slide forward on an empty chamber while you were reloading. In the last instance, you're going to need to rack the slide and feed a round into the chamber from the top of the fresh magazine.

If you're sitting, you may be able to accomplish this by pinching the gun between your knees (upright this time, muzzle clear of your knees and feet and pointing in a safe direction), and racking the slide with your one good hand. If you're standing, you will need to look for a solid surface on which you can snag the rear sights—your belt, holster edge, the side of a table, the heel of your boot, even the side of a crutch—pulling firmly to rack the slide using that surface.

Even if the slide on my semi-auto is locked open after firing the gun dry, I actually prefer to rack the slide if at all possible. Why? Because you don't get the extra fraction of an

Tacking a slide while one-handed is entirely possible. You can use the heel of your shoe, the rail of a walker or crutch, and even your own belt or exterior pocket—anything on which you can snag the rear sights and pull back the slide to release (just remember to be cognizant of your muzzle direction). Courtesy of Mike Seeklander.

inch tension on the spring using the slide stop with the slide held in its locked position, and so you do have an increased chance that the gun will fail to go completely into battery, which means not only can you not shoot, but now you have to clear a malfunction—one-handed.

Revolvers—Revolvers can require a bit more work to reload with one hand, but mostly because the cylinder release is always on the left side of the gun and the cylinder always rocks out to the left (with the exception of single-action revolvers and the older top-break models, neither of which would generally be recommended for self-defense purposes). Too, some cylinder releases push forward to activate (S&Ws), some merely push in (Rugers), and others are tugged to the rear (Colt), so a simple change in the grip, if you're challenged by being able to use only your left hand, can make operating the release anywhere from problematic to nearly impossible.

That said, if you can manipulate the cylinder release without letting go of your grip, do it. Otherwise, brace the gun in a manner so that, when you manipulate the cylinder release, the cylinder breaks free of its locking mechanism and releases out of the frame. In other words, do not lay a revolver on its right side, activate the cylinder release, and expect the cylinder to fall open when you pick the gun up. It likely won't. Therefore, you will need to pinch the gun at least semi-upright and preferably canted to the left, so that the cylinder will begin to fall away from the frame when its release is activated.

Swing out the cylinder fully, then tilt the muzzle and let the empty cases fall out. Do what you have to in order to depress the ejector rod and eject any stuck cases   push the revolver's ejector rod against your walker edge, a table edge, your holster edge, whatever works—but avoid allowing the cylinder to close up, which would mitigate starting the process over again.

Keeping the gun pinched or otherwise oriented so that the cylinder remains open, find your speedloader and quickly but carefully place it over the empty chambers, push the button, and release the cartridges. You'll have a better chance of having this reload go well if the revolver is angled down a bit and you let gravity help the cartridges enter their respective chambers. Toss your speedloader (forget about it just like you would an empty magazine from a semi-auto), and quickly hand load any cartridges that missed their mark. Now, swing the cylinder up and lock it into the frame, pick up the gun, and prepare to shoot again.

One note on cylinder closure. Most revolver owners know that you should never just flick your wrist to close up the cylinder, rather your thumb and/or hand should smoothly lift the cylinder up from its extended position and push it into the frame to lock it in place. That Hollywood, flicking-your-wrist move can quickly damage your revolver's crane (also called a "yoke" by some manufacturers, this is the part that swings out and supports the cylinder when it is out from the frame), eventually causing problems with cylinder lockup, rotation, and accuracy. However, if you're in an emergency situation, you may need to perform exactly that kind of move. Keep in mind that because the cylinder on a modern double-action revolver always extends to the left, the move can be awkward for left-handed shooting and send the cartridges flying out of their chambers before you can get the cylinder locked in place. Again, practice, practice, and more practice is the key; just be cautious of damaging the gun in the process, performing that wrist-flick move more gently than you would in a heated situation.

If you're uncomfortable flicking the cylinder of your revolver closed, simply wedge the muzzle between something (you and your other arm's cast, between your knees, in your holster, in your waistband, etc.), close the cylinder up with your good hand, and reassume your grip (always with your finger off the trigger). You can even just grip the revolver and press the cylinder closed against the side of your knee, a table, etc. I also Googled "one-handed revolver reloading" and found two useful YouTube videos by someone named

Allie Frick. Allie, who had an arm amputated after an accident, writes a blog called the One Arm Chick (onearmchick. blogspot.com). Worth watching—she was even successful in obtaining her concealed carry permit—and it really goes to show what creativity in the face of adversity can do for you.

Dealing with Firearm Malfunctions While One-Handed

Clearing malfunctions in a semi-auto doesn't work much differently than reloading one does. Malfunctions common to one-handed shooting include empty cases stove-piping and getting stuck in the ejection port, and live rounds not quite feeding into the chamber from the magazine. Both are generally the result of an unstable shooting platform on the part of the human (i.e., a wrist not strong enough to maintain a proper grip on the gun). One way to compensate for this is to cant the gun slightly toward the center. Ten to 30 degrees is more than adequate to reinforce your wrist. Especially in a dire situation where your adrenaline is pumping and you are perhaps shaking uncontrollably, both malfunctions will be the result of the slide not cycling to its full extent. Of course, the same malfunctions can occur if your gun disfavors a certain type of ammo—but you should have figured out what your gun likes with time on the range and lots of different ammo before you decided on the type and brand you loaded in your gun for self-defense purposes.

If either a stove-piped empty case or incomplete loading malfunction occurs while you're shooting, you will need to rack the slide. Use the same instructions as if reloading apply, just be very certain that your finger is on the frame and off the trigger during your actions.

Malfunctions in revolvers will almost certainly prove more difficult to remedy. Now, many people choose revolvers for self-defense specifically because they *aren't* prone to the handling mistake malfunctions of semi-autos; you can "limp wrist" a revolver all day long, and while you won't make the most accurate shot, the gun *will* fire. Still, as reliable as they are, revolvers can and do malfunction.

Your most common malfunction will be a cartridge not discharging. No problem, just pull the trigger and fire the next round in line.

Your second-most common malfunction will be an empty case stuck in the chamber when you go to reload. To solve this problem, bang the ejector rod hard, but make every effort to do this pounding at a straight angle so as not to damage the rod or the crane (yoke), which could prevent the cylinder from closing up. Can't unstick that empty case? Skip it, but then eject your live rounds from your speedloader into your lap or near you so that they don't roll away from you, then insert them one at a time into the chambers that are empty. Now, close the cylinder and prepare to shoot.

The worst-case scenario with a revolver is a failure for the cylinder to open. This most often occurs with "pulled" cartridges. Usually associated with big-bore, heavy recoiling revolvers, a pulled cartridge is one where recoil from previously fired cartridges has, literally, caused the bullet to be pulled forward and out of its case. This will prevent not only the cylinder from opening, but from turning. A backed out primer on a fired cartridge can produce the same results, just as can heavy carbon and residue buildup on an extremely dirty gun.

In all but the pulled cartridge instance, the correction will be to bang hard on the right side of the cylinder while maintaining activation of the cylinder release. The problem when you're a one-handed shooter is that this is most likely impossible; at least, I can't think of a way to do this one-handed. (Most revolver practitioners who experience a stuck cylinder will put the gun in a true vise, then activate their cylinder release button with one hand while banging on the cylinder with a mallet from the right side and forcing it out.) Therefore, if you have any reason to believe that your revolver is prone to having its cylinder stuck in place, either replace that firearm with one more reliable for self-defense, or ensure you maintain a backup firearm on or about you.

Dummy Rounds are Smart

Like so many defensive techniques, reloading and correcting firearms malfunctions while one-handed will run the gamut from awkward to difficult to near impossible. You'll never get proficient at these corrections without practice, but because their level of difficulty is elevated beyond that when two hands are employed, it's best to use empty magazines and dummy rounds until you are completely confident you can perform these corrections without your finger touching the trigger or having the muzzle sweep any unintended target—including your own body parts—while you're maneuvering the gun. I would even suggest you practice your reloading and malfunction corrections using an empty gun and dummy rounds while a knowledgeable friend watches you. Sometimes you can't see where you've violated a safety rule when you're so completely focused on a task like this using just one hand. That extra set of eyes can help you correct such infractions and even suggest another, better way of doing something.

In addition to compensating for an actual injury, you should also practice these skills when you have the use of all your body parts. Replicate a stove-piped case by sticking an empty case in the ejection port and correct the situation using only one hand. Reload your guns with only one hand, tying the other behind your back or putting it in a sling if you have to in order to keep from using it—and make sure you practice these skills with each hand individually, as well as practice them sitting, standing, kneeling, and prone, because you never know what a situation will force you to do in defense of your life. When you are injured or recovering from a debilitating illness, remember, too, to practice carefully, gradually building your strength and confidence. The last thing you need to do while injured is to cause more damage or injure additional body parts. That defeats the purpose of self-defense! It takes time to get comfortable, to get stronger, and to build your stamina when you are recovering, and you don't want to put yourself at risk until you are ready to move forward with confidence.

12. On Wheels

My friend Laurie is a funny, beautiful, smart firearms instructor who happens to be in a wheelchair. She was an active and avid shooter before the accident that changed her life, and, while admitting that it can be a bit more challenging now, she still enjoys many of the things she always has.

Being on wheels has not diminished Laurie's love of shooting, her zest for life, or her indomitable sense of humor.

When we first met, I asked Laurie if it was okay to ask what happened. She responded, completely straight-faced, that she had fallen off a stripper pole.

She's good. She lasted about forty-five seconds before she started laughing. It seemed like minutes to me, though, while I was attempting to formulate a response. She was teasing, of course, and, I think, getting a read of me at the same time. (She did tell me briefly, what happened, but she is really quite private about that aspect of her life—though I can tell you that it wasn't at all about a stripper pole.)

Laurie explained that the biggest difference for her in shooting post-accident is the loss of her core muscle strength. Depending on the location of a spinal injury, you lose more or less of the abdominal support that keeps us upright. That same support helps stabilize you while shooting.

Laurie does carry openly when she is teaching, although she admits that it can get in the way a little. She also keeps a compact firearm in a pocket holster tucked under her wheel-chair's cushion. She admits her everyday carry is generally concealed, more appendix oriented, and that often she will have a backup firearm in an ankle holster.

It never hurts to have a backup gun.

One of the biggest personal defense challenges Laurie is prepared for is getting dumped out of her chair. It was that consideration that led to the ankle carry as a quick-access backup. The possibility of being dumped from her chair also means she has had to learn to fall safely and recover quickly. This is a critical skill, and best learned from a professional experienced in training firearms self-defense for people in wheelchairs.

Another major point of vulnerability for someone in a wheelchair is the transfer in or out of the car. It can be a challenge to collapse and move the chair while maintaining awareness. Laurie, understanding this, takes care to fully assess her environment prior to initiating the transition.

Laurie admits she tires more quickly when shooting, but she still enjoys it. She will sometimes lean against the edge of the booth to help stabilize herself, but because that isn't always available and similar support certainly may not be available should she need to defend herself, she also practices shooting without the aid.

Laurie demonstrates how to shoot while leaning against a booth.

These were just some of the things we discussed about self-defense when you're in a wheelchair, and I learned a lot from our discussion. Perhaps the thing I most appreciated about her is that all the physical changes in her life hadn't impacted her sense of humor, her

Laurie shooting.

openness, or her love of shooting—and I also learned, after watching her, that I wouldn't want to be the fool who tried to mug her.

Bottom line here is that, as long as you can find a way to hold the gun and handle it safely, you can enjoy shooting. Laurie is an inspirational person, with her big smile and her obvious joy in the sport. She reminds us that almost anyone can shoot for fun and carry a gun for personal defense.

Part III
In the Thick of It

13. The Fight is On—What to Expect

When all else fails and you are in a struggle for your life, you need to know that you have practiced and prepared to the best of your abilities. You haven't prepared if you haven't thought about what you are willing to do, and without training, even the biggest, strongest, and toughest humans can crumple like tissue when adrenaline hits.

There are several well-documented physical responses to the stress of an imminent threat. Adrenaline dumps into your system, which can give you strength and focus. Meanwhile, your body diverts blood flow away from skin and internal organs and toward your head and the muscles of your extremities in an involuntary self-defense mechanism.

You may experience a time distortion during a threatening situation. This is called "tachypsychia," and it is a neurological response that makes things seem to move much faster or slower than normal. For me, things slow down in very high-stress situations, and that appears to be the more common response. But the opposite may also happen. If you don't know how *you* respond, you're going to be surprised by the sensation, and that isn't a good thing. It can be very disorienting.

Your field of vision may narrow—the tunnel vision you so often hear about—so that you are focused completely on the danger in front of you. When this happens, you will need to force yourself past this and scan for other threats—as well as innocent bystanders that could potentially be in your line of fire—that may be near but not in your direct line of vision.

Your hearing may become extremely focused and diminish. Called "auditory exclusion," it, too, is a neurological response to stress. Auditory exclusion may make sounds seem muffled, though you may be temporarily unable to hear at all. This can be a problem when the police arrive, especially when coupled with all that adrenaline and, perhaps, tunnel vision. You must, *must,* despite any of these physical responses happening to you, do everything you can to reorient your focus to take in as much information as possible. That muffled shouting you hear, is that coming from a partner of your attacker or the police? You can't just shoot willy-nilly at the noise.

While these stress responses can happen to anyone, and can happen singularly or in combination, the best defense against having them occur is with training. Let me give you, perhaps oddly enough, a non-defensive example.

I used to sing with a Sweet Adeline's chorus, a women's barbershop group. Our director was very good, and we went to several regional and international competitions. Knowing that being on stage in front of fifteen thousand people can be stressful, she drilled into us to "sing the plan." That turned out to be a good insight for me when I sang the National Anthem at a semi-pro football game and the broadcast through the arena's audio speakers was delayed behind my actual voice by about a second. Because of my chorus training, I was able to tune out what I was hearing and "sing the plan," getting through the song without being thrown off by the feedback from the lagging audio.

The same goes for self-defense. Work your plan. If your brain is throwing out all kinds of crazy impulses and nothing looks, sounds, or feels right, and if you have trained and are as prepared as you can be, you will revert to what you practiced. Having that plan, and practicing, can save your life.

14. To Shoot or Not to Shoot

A common question that comes up when we talk about being in a gunfight is that of when you should actually shoot. When do you pull the trigger? When do you wait?

There aren't really any hard rules or line-in-the-sand answers to those questions, as the decision (and justification) to pull the trigger will vary with every situation, but there are some considerations that should help you sort through the choices in a critical and chaotic situation.

First, and perhaps most important, ask yourself this: Are you in imminent threat of death or bodily harm? Imminent means *immediate*. Not tomorrow, not next week, maybe not even in the next five minutes, but right *now*. If the answer is "No," then you don't shoot. You cannot justify self-defense if you (or a loved one) are not in immediate danger.

Another serious consideration is that of who is around you. What's your environment like? If you are in a crowd of innocent people, the risk of injuring or killing a bystander(s) may outweigh your option to shoot.

Is the threat directed at you or someone else? This comes up a lot. Say you pull up to a convenience store and see someone pointing a gun at the clerk. Is this a robbery? Will you be rushing in to save the clerk? Or, is it a plain-clothes police officer arresting the clerk? How can you tell? You can't. Memorize the scene, leave, call the police, and be a good witness. No Shoot.

As much as I hate to admit it, women can be aggressors. There have been cases where a woman was attempting to assault a man, and when things didn't go her way she started screaming and begging for help in an effort to confuse onlookers into thinking she was the victim. Get away, call the police. No Shoot.

Are you seeing a pattern here? You need clear justification, minimal risk to others, and you need to be certain of the situation before you pull the trigger.

Over-Penetration—A Real Concern

Over-penetration is a term that refers to a bullet that passes through an object, such as a person or wall, and keeps going, potentially into an unintended target.

This is a real risk for anyone firing a gun. Popular ammunition, especially round-nose "ball" ammunition, has the ability to penetrate all sorts of media—walls, car doors, people—and continue on for a significant distance. This risk is minimized, but not eliminated, by the use of defensive ammunitions that contain hollow point bullets, which are designed to expand on contact (creating a large wound channel). As they expand upon hitting their mark, they slow down. Think of it like a parachute in reverse.

Some defensive ammunition is designed to be "frangible," meaning it's designed to break apart on contact. The purpose of frangible ammunition is two-fold: It lowers or eliminates the chance of over-penetration, and it creates multiple wound channels. It has been reported that Federal Air Marshals extensively tested the popular Glaser Safety Slugs, a type of frangible ammunition, during the seventies and eighties. Glaser Safety Slugs wear a plastic cap instead of a bullet. That cap holds a small load of very small shot pellets. Other frangible ammunition options are produced by SinterFire (projectiles only, not loaded ammunition; www.sinterfire.com), Dynamic Research Technologies (www.drtammo.com), ICC Ammo (www.iccammo. com), and others. They can be viable and smarter options for apartment, condo, and townhouse dwellers, as well as for use when staying in hotels; however, it is critical to be aware of direction and what is close as there are no guarantees. Many frangible ammunition options are also lead-free, making them usable on ranges that impose restrictions on the use of traditional ammo.

Remember the NSSF Safety Rules listed in the early part of this book? One of those states you should know your target and what is beyond it.

Over-penetration is why that rule is important (and another reason why you do not want your child directly behind you when confronted by a gunman).

If you load ammo specifically designed for self-defense in your carry firearm, you should also practice with it. Brands and varying loads (powder charges and bullet weights) within a caliber will fire and feel differently. Too, not all guns either work or work accurately with all ammunition designed for their caliber. Some semi-autos can be particularly persnickety about the ammunition they'll feed reliably (revolvers, of course, will fire any caliber meant for them, so that's not your concern, but every revolver likely favors particular brands and loads when it comes to accuracy). The time to find out whether your chosen ammunition works in your gun is at the range, not when your life depends on it. Think of it this way: The accepted malfunction rate with defensive ammunition should be *zero*. If a particular defensive ammunition doesn't feed well in your gun or doesn't go where you aim it, give it away and try a different brand.

As far how that defensive ammo feels, yes, you need to practice with it. You won't do the majority of your practice with it—that's what the less-expensive ball ammunition is for. But you should include a magazine or cylinder or two of self-defense ammo in your training runs every other time or so you go to the range. Just like you don't want to find out your gun doesn't feed an ammunition well when you need to defend yourself, you also don't want to find out that the round you've chosen has a lot more recoil than you're used to or that it's inaccurate.

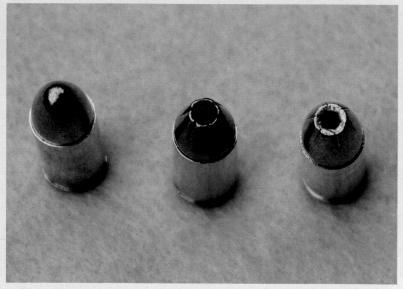

Practice round, hollow point with polymer tip, and hollow point ammo.

15. Defensive Shooting is Not Target Shooting

Defensive shooting techniques vary significantly from target shooting. When we first learn to shoot a handgun, most of us are taught the Isosceles stance, where your feet are about roughly shoulder width apart and parallel to each other, and your arms are straight out. Together, the stance can be seen to form a triangle, thus the name.

The Isosceles stance is great for a beginner and for a target shooter. It puts the sights squarely in front of their eyes and provides a stable platform from which to fire the gun and have it both function correctly and hit where the shooter is aiming.

The problem with the Isosceles stance is that it can be challenging to move quickly. You are in what can feel like a locked position. You can twist at the waist, but only so far, as your feet and legs are in that rigid position. Your legs are also rigid at the knees, and that makes for a stiffer, more awkward move if you need to walk or run in any direction. As you build strength and muscle memory and move on to defensive practice, you'll need to change this shooting stance.

Note the triangle formed by the fully extended arms and squared shoulders, supported by feet firmly placed about shoulder width apart.

For defensive shooting, you'll need to adopt more of a fighting stance, where one foot is slightly behind the other and your knees are slightly bent. This is what gives you the freedom to move quickly.

Beware of crossing your feet when you move, as this can obviously trip you up, and do not back up, if possible, unless you know exactly what is behind you. It's too easy to trip on a curb or other obstacle, causing you to fall, and if you look behind you, your focus is no longer on your attacker nor on where the muzzle of your firearm is oriented.

Such shooting stances are easy to practice at the range, and even at home if you're using a dummy blue gun or SIRT dummy gun. You can practice rolling on the ground while drawing, running from one position to another and shooting, reloading on the run, and other defensive techniques. If you have a partner, you can also practice more complex drills (many of which are detailed in my book *Female and Armed*), that include fighting off an attacker and drawing from dangerous positions.

Safe practice is key to any of these techniques—I cannot emphasize that enough. Anything you do with a firearm, dummy training gun or real, should be performed with the utmost care. If you are physically limited, you will need to discover

Defensive stance.

what you can do and then practice those things. And physically limited or not, if you are carrying concealed for defense, recognize that a defensive situation will rarely go down smoothly, and that it will be both chaotic and unpredictable. The better prepared you are and the more you have practiced, the more likely you will be able to survive the encounter.

Finally, and I talked about this early in the book, if you can get away, *do!* You do not want to put yourself in more danger than you have to, and you don't want to shoot someone if you don't have to.

Games to Hone Your Defensive Shooting Skills

There are three action-shooting sports that embrace the use of defensive shooting skills. They are, in order of complexity and gear requirements from least to most, IDPA (International Defensive Pistol Association), IPSC (International Practical Shooting Confederation) and its American body USPSA (United States Practical Shooting Association), and 3-Gun.

IDPA is a competitive forum that revolves around two kinds of matches, those with self-defense formats and those with standard shooting exercises designed to improve and hone basic skills. Shooters compete against others in their skill level, progressing as their talents evolve. The use of stock, factory-issued handguns is at the core of IDPA competition. That means no souped-up custom "speed" guns, and no fancy holsters, belts, or other equipment. Just bring your gun, eye and ear protection, ammo, a basic holster and belt, and magazines or speedloaders to any match and you're in. (www.idpa.com.)

IPSC/USPSA is rather a step up from IDPA, but don't let that intimidate you. Matches here are all about self-defense and tactical setups—there are often cars to get out of, barricade ports to shoot through and around, targets that can't be engaged without shooting other targets first, shoot/don't shoot targets, and usually lots of running around.

You'll also have steel plate knock-down speed stages where, literally, the fastest draw wins, as well as qualifier stages that work to set the bar for basic skills in a manner similar to the standard shooting exercises of IDPA. What IPSC offers that IDPA doesn't is the ability to trick out your gun and compete against others with similar firearms and ammunition. There are two classes within IPSC/USPSA, Limited and Open, and two "power factors" within each, Minor and Major. Limited is for what you might imagine, mostly factory stock guns, with few custom modifications allowed. Open is the opposite—if you can put it on a gun, including optics, then have at it. Minor is for lesser-powered, lower velocity cartridges meeting a certain pressure threshold and a maximum bullet diameter of less than 10mm (.400-inch); 9mm is your most common round. Major is higher-pressured and faster, those hot .38 Super and 10mm loads, and most .45 ACPs and .40 S&W loads. The sport is an absolute ball, but get into the sport and you'll need a specialty holster, belt, and plenty of magazines to shoot the game and win your class. In other words, IPSC/USPSA usually ends up being more gear-intensive than IDPA. (www.ipsc.org; www.uspsa.org.)

The king of action shooting sports is 3-Gun. Think of it as IPSC on steroids. You will shoot three guns in any match—shotgun, rifle, and handgun—and there are multiple equipment classes ranging from those that use stock military firearms to the same kind of tricked-out guns you'll find in IPSC's Open class (www.3gunnation.com).

The one thing all three of these sports have in common is self-defense. In fact, as challenging and outlandish as some of these matches get (at least one famous 3-Gun match has included the use of a zip line, and one 3-Gun match is entirely dedicated to night-shooting), they still have defensive tactics and moves at their cores. They can be excellent practice for the self-defense practitioner, not just because of those skills, but also because they're a tremendous amount of fun. That fun, more importantly, gets you practicing, plus you get the benefits of shooting under the pressure of competition, including right next to some of the world's very best shots. Yes, that's a different kind of stress than you'd experience in a fight for your life, but the "fun" stress can still improve your gun handling abilities. Plus, these competitions really kind of force you to get more and more familiar with your firearms as you go along, and that's certainly what will help keep you alive in a life-or-death situation.

16. The Best Confrontation and What to Do After

If you have read any of my other works, you know that I believe very strongly that the best confrontation is the one you don't have. Planning, awareness, and instinct can minimize your risk of a confrontation, but, if you find yourself in a situation in which you *may* need to defend your life with deadly force, the next best step is to minimize contact and do what you have to so that you can get away.

If you are in a physical confrontation, the odds are very high that you will suffer injury—or worse. Avoid this situation if at all possible. If you are able to get away, do so. Get to a safe place and call the police. She who calls first is often the one who is more likely to be believed, at least initially. Provide as much information as possible, including when, where, what, and descriptions. It's better to have the police looking for the wanna-be mugger who may be trolling for an easier victim than to have them looking for "the crazy lady screaming in the parking lot" that someone else phoned in.

If you are forced to use your firearm in self-defense you will likely have adrenaline, impaired memory, and some or all of the physical responses I talked about in an earlier chapter. However, know that, if you shoot and connect with your attacker, you are not required to provide first aid to them. In fact, watch your attacker closely, as being shot doesn't mean they're out of the fight. Do *not* approach them, do *not* engage them, and do *not* put down your firearm—get away if you can to safer place. Call the police if you haven't been able to already and try to stay calm, treating your own injuries if needed.

Once the police arrive, you will need to cooperate. In doing so, the first thing you need to understand is that they're walking into your situation blind. They don't know for sure, even with descriptions you or a witness may have proved them, who's the victim and who's the attacker, but they do know at least one of you has a gun—and if it's you standing there with someone else injured or dead on the ground, they're going to quickly understand it's you.

Every law enforcement officer's first concern is for their own life, even as they're coming to your aid. When they tell you to put down your gun, you do it. Do it slowly, carefully, deliberately—even tell them out loud that you are setting it down, and do so slowly, finger on the frame, and then move out of reach of it once it's on the ground. If they want to take your gun from you, stay still and let them. Follow *every* instruction they give you until they have determined you are the victim and the scene is secured.

You may be stunned to be find that *you* might be treated like a criminal suspect at first. You may be handcuffed, led away, and sat in a cruiser, while the officers work to sort things out. They may question you harshly if the scene is a complex one and what happened is unclear. *Expect* to be treated like a criminal, not a victim, at least until they can figure out what happened. Be courteous, be compliant, do not argue or resist.

Except for being compliant with instructions and answering basic questions such as your name and address, remain quiet and answer "what happened" questions minimally.

Adrenaline tends to impact the mouth, causing things to come out before the brain engages. The results can be accurate, partially accurate, or nonsensical—remember, you are under a *tremendous* amount of stress and are only *beginning* to process all that has happened to you. You've heard the Miranda warning "anything you say can and will be used against you"? Don't give the police something you will need to contradict later. Stay with the minimums, such as there was a second person who was wearing whatever, he came at me, I was in fear for my life, I thought he was going to kill me, I believe I require medical attention, etc. You also want to speak up promptly and request to speak with an attorney.

Speaking of attorneys, I encourage you to hire one after a deadly force incident, even if it's just to help you understand your rights and you don't end up needing them in a criminal proceeding. This will not be cheap—but weigh that expense against spending time in jail and the interruption to your job and household. In all actuality, the time to find a good gun attorney is *before* you need one. There are many organizations offering self-defense insurance. Some of these, such as the one offered by the United States Concealed Carry Association (www.usconcealedcarry.com) are arranged as a shared fund that cover costs for those partaking in the policy (or membership) if they become involved in a self-defense shooting. Others are individual policies, such as the one endorsed by the NRA (www.mynrainsurance.com). As with any insurance product, do your research before you buy.

The final thing to understand if you are in a confrontation and, in the end, are talking to the police or your attorney, is that you escaped. You won! It doesn't matter if you used all your skills or you forgot everything, shoved them and ran. You won, you did what you needed to do. Do not second-guess yourself or feel bad that you didn't remember to do something in plan. That is all very normal, and can happen to any well-trained individual. If you fell back on instinct, it is okay, you survived, you are okay—and I'll say it again, you *won*.

Part IV
General Considerations for
Carriers of Firearms

17. Safe Storage

Part of having a gun at home means having a safe place to keep it. Ideally, you want a locking container that still gives you quick access. There are many models of safes for single, individual guns, as well as furniture with secret compartments, that make ideal places to secure a gun. If you have a large or multi-level home, you may want more than one option strategically placed around the home.

My preference is for the containers that have what looks like a handprint on the top to guide your fingers into place so you can easily work the cypher combination, even in the dark. There are also handgun safes out there that have a biometric lock, where you pass your index finger over a sensor. I'm not comfortable that this technology is as foolproof as the physical cypher combination yet, but it is certainly another option to consider.

The quick-access safes meant for storing one handgun are likely going to be your smartest choice for keeping that firearm accessible for self-defense in the home, under your control, and away from access by unauthorized individuals. This includes those of you who are single—no need to lose your gun to a burglary—but these small safes are especially important for households with children. If you believe in keeping a gun for self-defense in your home, most people would want that gun to be loaded, for doing so saves time in an emergency situation and prevents fumbling for magazines or speedloaders in the dark. But you cannot keep a loaded gun in your home (or your car, or anywhere else except on your person and in your immediate control), without preventing unauthorized access to it. That means all children most of all, but it also means guests to your home and service people and utility workers who might enter your dwelling.

Of course, in my experience, there are few gun owners who have just a single firearm. Let's face it, they're like potato chips, once you get started. The joke is "How many guns do I need? One more than I have!" That said, when the collection warrants it, you should invest in a secure storage cabinet or safe. You should also store your firearms and ammunition separately, just in case.

With larger floor safes, it is important to have a form of desiccant, or de-humidifier, in that safe. Desiccant is available in packets that you will need to replace from time to time. Many people with floor model safes use electric dehumidifiers. Either work to cut down on the humidity inside the safe, thereby minimizing the risk of rust attacking

Gun vault.

your firearms. Guns are expensive. Take good care of them, clean them regularly, store them properly, and they will last a lifetime and more.

Project ChildSafe

The Project ChildSafe program was developed by the National Shooting Sports Foundation® (NSSF®), the trade association for the firearms industry. It is a non-profit, 501(c)(3) charitable organization that, according to its website, www.projectchildsafe.org, "is committed to promoting fire-arms safety among firearms owners through the distribution of safety education messages and free firearm safety kits. The kits include a cable-style gun-locking device and brochure (also available in Spanish) that discusses safe handling and secure storage guidelines to help deter access by unauthor-ized individuals."

Project ChildSafe has touched all fifty states and all five U.S. territories through its work with more than 15,000 law enforcement agencies in their home communities. Partnered with NSSF's "Own it? Respect it. Secure it." initiative that works through firearms retailers and other industry members to help spread the word about safe and responsible gun storage, the Project ChildSafe initiative has distributed more than thirty-six million safety kits.

To learn more, including how you can help support this important cause, visit www.projectchildsafe.org. There you'll find tips and videos on safe firearms handling and storage, information on partners working with Project ChildSafe, upcoming Project ChildSafe events, and much more.

Gun Locks

Cable-style locks, like those that come in the Project ChildSafe Safety Kit, should be used in addition to— not as a substitute for—safe firearms handling and storage methods. Another popular lock style is the clam-shell type that locks around the trigger guard and secures with a physical key, and a new company on the scene, Omega Gun Lock, manufactures a device that, when placed inside the gun's action, locks the chamber and prevents it from being loaded. All of these locks are intended to discourage unauthorized access to a firearm, particularly by young children, but none should be considered high-security devices.

Afterword

Writing a book is a lot like a leap of faith. You start out with an idea, expand on it, and then try to build it into something that people will read and appreciate. It is the hardest and most rewarding thing I've ever done.

Along the path of this book, I met a lot of amazing people who were generous with their time and knowledge and personal stories. My sincere appreciation goes out to each of them. I especially want to thank Judith Roth for introducing me to many of these people, and for gamely trying everything I asked her to do for photographs (and for introducing me to my first pastrami sandwich at a little deli in Virginia Beach).

In writing this book, I realized how lucky I am to be as mobile as I am. As I was inventorying my various aches and injuries, I realized that I really need to thank my orthopedic surgeon, Dr. Tom Martinelli, for the excellent care he has given me over the past few decades, as well as the encouragement to push through the recovery process each time. He's helped to make me as able as I can be.

I also need to thank the wonderful friends who patiently listened to ideas and concepts and provided feedback to help me bring this book home.

Finally, I need to thank the amazing man in my life, who understood when I needed to lock myself in a room to write and who listened and supported me through this journey.

I hope the suggestions and tips you've read within these pages offer you encouragement and a sense of control when you feel out of control. I hope that this book helps you realize that, no matter what, you are your own best defense, and that you have the right and the ability to protect yourself and your family no matter what your age or physical condition. Be strong, be secure, and be safe!

—Lynne Finch

About the Author

L ynne Finch holds multiple NRA instructor creden-
tials, including Refuse to be a Victim, as well as being
a SabreRed Pepper Spray instructor and a Defensive
Firearms Coach. Her first book, *Taking Your First Shot*,
addressed defensive shooting for women. In her second
book, *The Home Security Handbook*, she continues talking
about safety by including ideas and tips for keeping you and
your family out of harm's way. Her third book, *Female and
Armed* addresses more advanced defensive techniques. Finch
authors a popular blog, FemaleandArmed, as well as being
a contributing writer for *Gun Shows Today* and *Combat
Handgun Magazine*. Finch's training company, Female and
Armed, is located in Northern Virginia, where she resides
with her two adorable rescue cats, Rhiannon and Cinnia.